C-2065   CAREER EXAMINATION SERIES

This is your
PASSBOOK for...

Supervising Janitor

Test Preparation Study Guide
Questions & Answers

NATIONAL LEARNING CORPORATION®

COPYRIGHT NOTICE

This book is SOLELY intended for, is sold ONLY to, and its use is RESTRICTED to individual, bona fide applicants or candidates who qualify by virtue of having seriously filed applications for appropriate license, certificate, professional and/or promotional advancement, higher school matriculation, scholarship, or other legitimate requirements of education and/or governmental authorities.

This book is NOT intended for use, class instruction, tutoring, training, duplication, copying, reprinting, excerption, or adaptation, etc., by:

1) Other publishers
2) Proprietors and/or Instructors of "Coaching" and/or Preparatory Courses
3) Personnel and/or Training Divisions of commercial, industrial, and governmental organizations
4) Schools, colleges, or universities and/or their departments and staffs, including teachers and other personnel
5) Testing Agencies or Bureaus
6) Study groups which seek by the purchase of a single volume to copy and/or duplicate and/or adapt this material for use by the group as a whole without having purchased individual volumes for each of the members of the group
7) Et al.

Such persons would be in violation of appropriate Federal and State statutes.

PROVISION OF LICENSING AGREEMENTS – Recognized educational, commercial, industrial, and governmental institutions and organizations, and others legitimately engaged in educational pursuits, including training, testing, and measurement activities, may address request for a licensing agreement to the copyright owners, who will determine whether, and under what conditions, including fees and charges, the materials in this book may be used them. In other words, a licensing facility exists for the legitimate use of the material in this book on other than an individual basis. However, it is asseverated and affirmed here that the material in this book CANNOT be used without the receipt of the express permission of such a licensing agreement from the Publishers. Inquiries re licensing should be addressed to the company, attention rights and permissions department.

All rights reserved, including the right of reproduction in whole or in part, in any form or by any means, electronic or mechanical, including photocopying, recording, or by any information storage and retrieval system, without permission in writing from the Publisher.

Copyright © 2024 by
National Learning Corporation

212 Michael Drive, Syosset, NY 11791
(516) 921-8888 • www.passbooks.com
E-mail: info@passbooks.com

PUBLISHED IN THE UNITED STATES OF AMERICA

PASSBOOK® SERIES

THE *PASSBOOK® SERIES* has been created to prepare applicants and candidates for the ultimate academic battlefield – the examination room.

At some time in our lives, each and every one of us may be required to take an examination – for validation, matriculation, admission, qualification, registration, certification, or licensure.

Based on the assumption that every applicant or candidate has met the basic formal educational standards, has taken the required number of courses, and read the necessary texts, the *PASSBOOK® SERIES* furnishes the one special preparation which may assure passing with confidence, instead of failing with insecurity. Examination questions – together with answers – are furnished as the basic vehicle for study so that the mysteries of the examination and its compounding difficulties may be eliminated or diminished by a sure method.

This book is meant to help you pass your examination provided that you qualify and are serious in your objective.

The entire field is reviewed through the huge store of content information which is succinctly presented through a provocative and challenging approach – the question-and-answer method.

A climate of success is established by furnishing the correct answers at the end of each test.

You soon learn to recognize types of questions, forms of questions, and patterns of questioning. You may even begin to anticipate expected outcomes.

You perceive that many questions are repeated or adapted so that you can gain acute insights, which may enable you to score many sure points.

You learn how to confront new questions, or types of questions, and to attack them confidently and work out the correct answers.

You note objectives and emphases, and recognize pitfalls and dangers, so that you may make positive educational adjustments.

Moreover, you are kept fully informed in relation to new concepts, methods, practices, and directions in the field.

You discover that you are actually taking the examination all the time: you are preparing for the examination by "taking" an examination, not by reading extraneous and/or supererogatory textbooks.

In short, this PASSBOOK®, used directedly, should be an important factor in helping you to pass your test.

SUPERVISING JANITOR

DUTIES
Supervising Janitors supervise the care and cleaning of public buildings and grounds. In larger buildings, they supervise a large force of janitors, cleaners, and building service aides on an assigned shift. They check the operational condition of lights, heating and fire protection equipment, and plumbing fixtures. They distribute cleaning and maintenance supplies and supervise and/or perform minor maintenance repairs to buildings and equipment.

SCOPE OF EXAMINATION
The written test will be designed to test for knowledge, skills, and/or abilities in such areas as:
1. Building cleaning;
2. Ability to read follows written instructions;
3. Preparing written material; and
4. Supervision and training.

HOW TO TAKE A TEST

I. YOU MUST PASS AN EXAMINATION

A. *WHAT EVERY CANDIDATE SHOULD KNOW*

Examination applicants often ask us for help in preparing for the written test. What can I study in advance? What kinds of questions will be asked? How will the test be given? How will the papers be graded?

As an applicant for a civil service examination, you may be wondering about some of these things. Our purpose here is to suggest effective methods of advance study and to describe civil service examinations.

Your chances for success on this examination can be increased if you know how to prepare. Those "pre-examination jitters" can be reduced if you know what to expect. You can even experience an adventure in good citizenship if you know why civil service exams are given.

B. *WHY ARE CIVIL SERVICE EXAMINATIONS GIVEN?*

Civil service examinations are important to you in two ways. As a citizen, you want public jobs filled by employees who know how to do their work. As a job seeker, you want a fair chance to compete for that job on an equal footing with other candidates. The best-known means of accomplishing this two-fold goal is the competitive examination.

Exams are widely publicized throughout the nation. They may be administered for jobs in federal, state, city, municipal, town or village governments or agencies.

Any citizen may apply, with some limitations, such as the age or residence of applicants. Your experience and education may be reviewed to see whether you meet the requirements for the particular examination. When these requirements exist, they are reasonable and applied consistently to all applicants. Thus, a competitive examination may cause you some uneasiness now, but it is your privilege and safeguard.

C. *HOW ARE CIVIL SERVICE EXAMS DEVELOPED?*

Examinations are carefully written by trained technicians who are specialists in the field known as "psychological measurement," in consultation with recognized authorities in the field of work that the test will cover. These experts recommend the subject matter areas or skills to be tested; only those knowledges or skills important to your success on the job are included. The most reliable books and source materials available are used as references. Together, the experts and technicians judge the difficulty level of the questions.

Test technicians know how to phrase questions so that the problem is clearly stated. Their ethics do not permit "trick" or "catch" questions. Questions may have been tried out on sample groups, or subjected to statistical analysis, to determine their usefulness.

Written tests are often used in combination with performance tests, ratings of training and experience, and oral interviews. All of these measures combine to form the best-known means of finding the right person for the right job.

II. HOW TO PASS THE WRITTEN TEST

A. NATURE OF THE EXAMINATION

To prepare intelligently for civil service examinations, you should know how they differ from school examinations you have taken. In school you were assigned certain definite pages to read or subjects to cover. The examination questions were quite detailed and usually emphasized memory. Civil service exams, on the other hand, try to discover your present ability to perform the duties of a position, plus your potentiality to learn these duties. In other words, a civil service exam attempts to predict how successful you will be. Questions cover such a broad area that they cannot be as minute and detailed as school exam questions.

In the public service similar kinds of work, or positions, are grouped together in one "class." This process is known as *position-classification*. All the positions in a class are paid according to the salary range for that class. One class title covers all of these positions, and they are all tested by the same examination.

B. FOUR BASIC STEPS

1) Study the announcement

How, then, can you know what subjects to study? Our best answer is: "Learn as much as possible about the class of positions for which you've applied." The exam will test the knowledge, skills and abilities needed to do the work.

Your most valuable source of information about the position you want is the official exam announcement. This announcement lists the training and experience qualifications. Check these standards and apply only if you come reasonably close to meeting them.

The brief description of the position in the examination announcement offers some clues to the subjects which will be tested. Think about the job itself. Review the duties in your mind. Can you perform them, or are there some in which you are rusty? Fill in the blank spots in your preparation.

Many jurisdictions preview the written test in the exam announcement by including a section called "Knowledge and Abilities Required," "Scope of the Examination," or some similar heading. Here you will find out specifically what fields will be tested.

2) Review your own background

Once you learn in general what the position is all about, and what you need to know to do the work, ask yourself which subjects you already know fairly well and which need improvement. You may wonder whether to concentrate on improving your strong areas or on building some background in your fields of weakness. When the announcement has specified "some knowledge" or "considerable knowledge," or has used adjectives like "beginning principles of..." or "advanced ... methods," you can get a clue as to the number and difficulty of questions to be asked in any given field. More questions, and hence broader coverage, would be included for those subjects which are more important in the work. Now weigh your strengths and weaknesses against the job requirements and prepare accordingly.

3) Determine the level of the position

Another way to tell how intensively you should prepare is to understand the level of the job for which you are applying. Is it the entering level? In other words, is this the position in which beginners in a field of work are hired? Or is it an intermediate or advanced level? Sometimes this is indicated by such words as "Junior" or "Senior" in the class title. Other jurisdictions use Roman numerals to designate the level – Clerk I, Clerk II, for example. The word "Supervisor" sometimes appears in the title. If the level is not indicated by the title, check the description of duties. Will you be working under very close supervision, or will you have responsibility for independent decisions in this work?

4) Choose appropriate study materials

Now that you know the subjects to be examined and the relative amount of each subject to be covered, you can choose suitable study materials. For beginning level jobs, or even advanced ones, if you have a pronounced weakness in some aspect of your training, read a modern, standard textbook in that field. Be sure it is up to date and has general coverage. Such books are normally available at your library, and the librarian will be glad to help you locate one. For entry-level positions, questions of appropriate difficulty are chosen -- neither highly advanced questions, nor those too simple. Such questions require careful thought but not advanced training.

If the position for which you are applying is technical or advanced, you will read more advanced, specialized material. If you are already familiar with the basic principles of your field, elementary textbooks would waste your time. Concentrate on advanced textbooks and technical periodicals. Think through the concepts and review difficult problems in your field.

These are all general sources. You can get more ideas on your own initiative, following these leads. For example, training manuals and publications of the government agency which employs workers in your field can be useful, particularly for technical and professional positions. A letter or visit to the government department involved may result in more specific study suggestions, and certainly will provide you with a more definite idea of the exact nature of the position you are seeking.

III. KINDS OF TESTS

Tests are used for purposes other than measuring knowledge and ability to perform specified duties. For some positions, it is equally important to test ability to make adjustments to new situations or to profit from training. In others, basic mental abilities not dependent on information are essential. Questions which test these things may not appear as pertinent to the duties of the position as those which test for knowledge and information. Yet they are often highly important parts of a fair examination. For very general questions, it is almost impossible to help you direct your study efforts. What we can do is to point out some of the more common of these general abilities needed in public service positions and describe some typical questions.

1) General information

Broad, general information has been found useful for predicting job success in some kinds of work. This is tested in a variety of ways, from vocabulary lists to questions about current events. Basic background in some field of work, such as sociology or economics, may be sampled in a group of questions. Often these are principles which have become familiar to most persons through exposure rather than through formal training. It is difficult to advise you how to study for these questions; being alert to the world around you is our best suggestion.

2) Verbal ability

An example of an ability needed in many positions is verbal or language ability. Verbal ability is, in brief, the ability to use and understand words. Vocabulary and grammar tests are typical measures of this ability. Reading comprehension or paragraph interpretation questions are common in many kinds of civil service tests. You are given a paragraph of written material and asked to find its central meaning.

3) Numerical ability

Number skills can be tested by the familiar arithmetic problem, by checking paired lists of numbers to see which are alike and which are different, or by interpreting charts and graphs. In the latter test, a graph may be printed in the test booklet which you are asked to use as the basis for answering questions.

4) Observation

A popular test for law-enforcement positions is the observation test. A picture is shown to you for several minutes, then taken away. Questions about the picture test your ability to observe both details and larger elements.

5) Following directions

In many positions in the public service, the employee must be able to carry out written instructions dependably and accurately. You may be given a chart with several columns, each column listing a variety of information. The questions require you to carry out directions involving the information given in the chart.

6) Skills and aptitudes

Performance tests effectively measure some manual skills and aptitudes. When the skill is one in which you are trained, such as typing or shorthand, you can practice. These tests are often very much like those given in business school or high school courses. For many of the other skills and aptitudes, however, no short-time preparation can be made. Skills and abilities natural to you or that you have developed throughout your lifetime are being tested.

Many of the general questions just described provide all the data needed to answer the questions and ask you to use your reasoning ability to find the answers. Your best preparation for these tests, as well as for tests of facts and ideas, is to be at your physical and mental best. You, no doubt, have your own methods of getting into an exam-taking mood and keeping "in shape." The next section lists some ideas on this subject.

IV. KINDS OF QUESTIONS

Only rarely is the "essay" question, which you answer in narrative form, used in civil service tests. Civil service tests are usually of the short-answer type. Full instructions for answering these questions will be given to you at the examination. But in case this is your first experience with short-answer questions and separate answer sheets, here is what you need to know:

1) Multiple-choice Questions

Most popular of the short-answer questions is the "multiple choice" or "best answer" question. It can be used, for example, to test for factual knowledge, ability to solve problems or judgment in meeting situations found at work.

A multiple-choice question is normally one of three types—
- It can begin with an incomplete statement followed by several possible endings. You are to find the one ending which *best* completes the statement, although some of the others may not be entirely wrong.
- It can also be a complete statement in the form of a question which is answered by choosing one of the statements listed.

- It can be in the form of a problem – again you select the best answer.

Here is an example of a multiple-choice question with a discussion which should give you some clues as to the method for choosing the right answer:

When an employee has a complaint about his assignment, the action which will *best* help him overcome his difficulty is to
- A. discuss his difficulty with his coworkers
- B. take the problem to the head of the organization
- C. take the problem to the person who gave him the assignment
- D. say nothing to anyone about his complaint

In answering this question, you should study each of the choices to find which is best. Consider choice "A" – Certainly an employee may discuss his complaint with fellow employees, but no change or improvement can result, and the complaint remains unresolved. Choice "B" is a poor choice since the head of the organization probably does not know what assignment you have been given, and taking your problem to him is known as "going over the head" of the supervisor. The supervisor, or person who made the assignment, is the person who can clarify it or correct any injustice. Choice "C" is, therefore, correct. To say nothing, as in choice "D," is unwise. Supervisors have and interest in knowing the problems employees are facing, and the employee is seeking a solution to his problem.

2) True/False Questions

The "true/false" or "right/wrong" form of question is sometimes used. Here a complete statement is given. Your job is to decide whether the statement is right or wrong.

SAMPLE: A roaming cell-phone call to a nearby city costs less than a non-roaming call to a distant city.

This statement is wrong, or false, since roaming calls are more expensive.

This is not a complete list of all possible question forms, although most of the others are variations of these common types. You will always get complete directions for answering questions. Be sure you understand *how* to mark your answers – ask questions until you do.

V. RECORDING YOUR ANSWERS

Computer terminals are used more and more today for many different kinds of exams.

For an examination with very few applicants, you may be told to record your answers in the test booklet itself. Separate answer sheets are much more common. If this separate answer sheet is to be scored by machine – and this is often the case – it is highly important that you mark your answers correctly in order to get credit.

An electronic scoring machine is often used in civil service offices because of the speed with which papers can be scored. Machine-scored answer sheets must be marked with a pencil, which will be given to you. This pencil has a high graphite content which responds to the electronic scoring machine. As a matter of fact, stray dots may register as answers, so do not let your pencil rest on the answer sheet while you are pondering the correct answer. Also, if your pencil lead breaks or is otherwise defective, ask for another.

Since the answer sheet will be dropped in a slot in the scoring machine, be careful not to bend the corners or get the paper crumpled.

The answer sheet normally has five vertical columns of numbers, with 30 numbers to a column. These numbers correspond to the question numbers in your test booklet. After each number, going across the page are four or five pairs of dotted lines. These short dotted lines have small letters or numbers above them. The first two pairs may also have a "T" or "F" above the letters. This indicates that the first two pairs only are to be used if the questions are of the true-false type. If the questions are multiple choice, disregard the "T" and "F" and pay attention only to the small letters or numbers.

Answer your questions in the manner of the sample that follows:

32. The largest city in the United States is
   A. Washington, D.C.
   B. New York City
   C. Chicago
   D. Detroit
   E. San Francisco

1) Choose the answer you think is best. (New York City is the largest, so "B" is correct.)
2) Find the row of dotted lines numbered the same as the question you are answering. (Find row number 32)
3) Find the pair of dotted lines corresponding to the answer. (Find the pair of lines under the mark "B.")
4) Make a solid black mark between the dotted lines.

VI. BEFORE THE TEST

Common sense will help you find procedures to follow to get ready for an examination. Too many of us, however, overlook these sensible measures. Indeed, nervousness and fatigue have been found to be the most serious reasons why applicants fail to do their best on civil service tests. Here is a list of reminders:

- Begin your preparation early – Don't wait until the last minute to go scurrying around for books and materials or to find out what the position is all about.
- Prepare continuously – An hour a night for a week is better than an all-night cram session. This has been definitely established. What is more, a night a week for a month will return better dividends than crowding your study into a shorter period of time.
- Locate the place of the exam – You have been sent a notice telling you when and where to report for the examination. If the location is in a different town or otherwise unfamiliar to you, it would be well to inquire the best route and learn something about the building.
- Relax the night before the test – Allow your mind to rest. Do not study at all that night. Plan some mild recreation or diversion; then go to bed early and get a good night's sleep.
- Get up early enough to make a leisurely trip to the place for the test – This way unforeseen events, traffic snarls, unfamiliar buildings, etc. will not upset you.
- Dress comfortably – A written test is not a fashion show. You will be known by number and not by name, so wear something comfortable.

- Leave excess paraphernalia at home – Shopping bags and odd bundles will get in your way. You need bring only the items mentioned in the official notice you received; usually everything you need is provided. Do not bring reference books to the exam. They will only confuse those last minutes and be taken away from you when in the test room.
- Arrive somewhat ahead of time – If because of transportation schedules you must get there very early, bring a newspaper or magazine to take your mind off yourself while waiting.
- Locate the examination room – When you have found the proper room, you will be directed to the seat or part of the room where you will sit. Sometimes you are given a sheet of instructions to read while you are waiting. Do not fill out any forms until you are told to do so; just read them and be prepared.
- Relax and prepare to listen to the instructions
- If you have any physical problem that may keep you from doing your best, be sure to tell the test administrator. If you are sick or in poor health, you really cannot do your best on the exam. You can come back and take the test some other time.

VII. AT THE TEST

The day of the test is here and you have the test booklet in your hand. The temptation to get going is very strong. Caution! There is more to success than knowing the right answers. You must know how to identify your papers and understand variations in the type of short-answer question used in this particular examination. Follow these suggestions for maximum results from your efforts:

1) Cooperate with the monitor

The test administrator has a duty to create a situation in which you can be as much at ease as possible. He will give instructions, tell you when to begin, check to see that you are marking your answer sheet correctly, and so on. He is not there to guard you, although he will see that your competitors do not take unfair advantage. He wants to help you do your best.

2) Listen to all instructions

Don't jump the gun! Wait until you understand all directions. In most civil service tests you get more time than you need to answer the questions. So don't be in a hurry Read each word of instructions until you clearly understand the meaning. Study the examples, listen to all announcements and follow directions. Ask questions if you do not understand what to do.

3) Identify your papers

Civil service exams are usually identified by number only. You will be assigned a number; you must not put your name on your test papers. Be sure to copy your number correctly. Since more than one exam may be given, copy your exact examination title.

4) Plan your time

Unless you are told that a test is a "speed" or "rate of work" test, speed itself is usually not important. Time enough to answer all the questions will be provided, but this does not mean that you have all day. An overall time limit has been set. Divide the total time (in minutes) by the number of questions to determine the approximate time you have for each question.

5) Do not linger over difficult questions

If you come across a difficult question, mark it with a paper clip (useful to have along) and come back to it when you have been through the booklet. One caution if you do this – be sure to skip a number on your answer sheet as well. Check often to be sure that you have not lost your place and that you are marking in the row numbered the same as the question you are answering.

6) Read the questions

Be sure you know what the question asks! Many capable people are unsuccessful because they failed to *read* the questions correctly.

7) Answer all questions

Unless you have been instructed that a penalty will be deducted for incorrect answers, it is better to guess than to omit a question.

8) Speed tests

It is often better NOT to guess on speed tests. It has been found that on timed tests people are tempted to spend the last few seconds before time is called in marking answers at random – without even reading them – in the hope of picking up a few extra points. To discourage this practice, the instructions may warn you that your score will be "corrected" for guessing. That is, a penalty will be applied. The incorrect answers will be deducted from the correct ones, or some other penalty formula will be used.

9) Review your answers

If you finish before time is called, go back to the questions you guessed or omitted to give them further thought. Review other answers if you have time.

10) Return your test materials

If you are ready to leave before others have finished or time is called, take ALL your materials to the monitor and leave quietly. Never take any test material with you. The monitor can discover whose papers are not complete, and taking a test booklet may be grounds for disqualification.

VIII. EXAMINATION TECHNIQUES

1) Read the general instructions carefully. These are usually printed on the first page of the exam booklet. As a rule, these instructions refer to the timing of the examination; the fact that you should not start work until the signal and must stop work at a signal, etc. If there are any *special* instructions, such as a choice of questions to be answered, make sure that you note this instruction carefully.

2) When you are ready to start work on the examination, that is as soon as the signal has been given, read the instructions to each question booklet, underline any key words or phrases, such as *least, best, outline, describe* and the like. In this way you will tend to answer as requested rather than discover on reviewing your paper that you *listed without describing*, that you selected the *worst* choice rather than the *best* choice, etc.

3) If the examination is of the objective or multiple-choice type – that is, each question will also give a series of possible answers: A, B, C or D, and you are called upon to select the best answer and write the letter next to that answer on your answer paper – it is advisable to start answering each question in turn. There may be anywhere from 50 to 100 such questions in the three or four hours allotted and you can see how much time would be taken if you read through all the questions before beginning to answer any. Furthermore, if you come across a question or group of questions which you know would be difficult to answer, it would undoubtedly affect your handling of all the other questions.

4) If the examination is of the essay type and contains but a few questions, it is a moot point as to whether you should read all the questions before starting to answer any one. Of course, if you are given a choice – say five out of seven and the like – then it is essential to read all the questions so you can eliminate the two that are most difficult. If, however, you are asked to answer all the questions, there may be danger in trying to answer the easiest one first because you may find that you will spend too much time on it. The best technique is to answer the first question, then proceed to the second, etc.

5) Time your answers. Before the exam begins, write down the time it started, then add the time allowed for the examination and write down the time it must be completed, then divide the time available somewhat as follows:
    - If 3-1/2 hours are allowed, that would be 210 minutes. If you have 80 objective-type questions, that would be an average of 2-1/2 minutes per question. Allow yourself no more than 2 minutes per question, or a total of 160 minutes, which will permit about 50 minutes to review.
    - If for the time allotment of 210 minutes there are 7 essay questions to answer, that would average about 30 minutes a question. Give yourself only 25 minutes per question so that you have about 35 minutes to review.

6) The most important instruction is to *read each question* and make sure you know what is wanted. The second most important instruction is to *time yourself properly* so that you answer every question. The third most important instruction is to *answer every question*. Guess if you have to but include something for each question. Remember that you will receive no credit for a blank and will probably receive some credit if you write something in answer to an essay question. If you guess a letter – say "B" for a multiple-choice question – you may have guessed right. If you leave a blank as an answer to a multiple-choice question, the examiners may respect your feelings but it will not add a point to your score. Some exams may penalize you for wrong answers, so in such cases *only*, you may not want to guess unless you have some basis for your answer.

7) Suggestions
    a. Objective-type questions
        1. Examine the question booklet for proper sequence of pages and questions
        2. Read all instructions carefully
        3. Skip any question which seems too difficult; return to it after all other questions have been answered
        4. Apportion your time properly; do not spend too much time on any single question or group of questions

5. Note and underline key words – *all, most, fewest, least, best, worst, same, opposite,* etc.
6. Pay particular attention to negatives
7. Note unusual option, e.g., unduly long, short, complex, different or similar in content to the body of the question
8. Observe the use of "hedging" words – *probably, may, most likely,* etc.
9. Make sure that your answer is put next to the same number as the question
10. Do not second-guess unless you have good reason to believe the second answer is definitely more correct
11. Cross out original answer if you decide another answer is more accurate; do not erase until you are ready to hand your paper in
12. Answer all questions; guess unless instructed otherwise
13. Leave time for review

   b. Essay questions
   1. Read each question carefully
   2. Determine exactly what is wanted. Underline key words or phrases.
   3. Decide on outline or paragraph answer
   4. Include many different points and elements unless asked to develop any one or two points or elements
   5. Show impartiality by giving pros and cons unless directed to select one side only
   6. Make and write down any assumptions you find necessary to answer the questions
   7. Watch your English, grammar, punctuation and choice of words
   8. Time your answers; don't crowd material

8) Answering the essay question

Most essay questions can be answered by framing the specific response around several key words or ideas. Here are a few such key words or ideas:

M's: manpower, materials, methods, money, management
P's: purpose, program, policy, plan, procedure, practice, problems, pitfalls, personnel, public relations

   a. Six basic steps in handling problems:
   1. Preliminary plan and background development
   2. Collect information, data and facts
   3. Analyze and interpret information, data and facts
   4. Analyze and develop solutions as well as make recommendations
   5. Prepare report and sell recommendations
   6. Install recommendations and follow up effectiveness

   b. Pitfalls to avoid
   1. *Taking things for granted* – A statement of the situation does not necessarily imply that each of the elements is necessarily true; for example, a complaint may be invalid and biased so that all that can be taken for granted is that a complaint has been registered

2. *Considering only one side of a situation* – Wherever possible, indicate several alternatives and then point out the reasons you selected the best one
3. *Failing to indicate follow up* – Whenever your answer indicates action on your part, make certain that you will take proper follow-up action to see how successful your recommendations, procedures or actions turn out to be
4. *Taking too long in answering any single question* – Remember to time your answers properly

IX. AFTER THE TEST

Scoring procedures differ in detail among civil service jurisdictions although the general principles are the same. Whether the papers are hand-scored or graded by machine we have described, they are nearly always graded by number. That is, the person who marks the paper knows only the number – never the name – of the applicant. Not until all the papers have been graded will they be matched with names. If other tests, such as training and experience or oral interview ratings have been given, scores will be combined. Different parts of the examination usually have different weights. For example, the written test might count 60 percent of the final grade, and a rating of training and experience 40 percent. In many jurisdictions, veterans will have a certain number of points added to their grades.

After the final grade has been determined, the names are placed in grade order and an eligible list is established. There are various methods for resolving ties between those who get the same final grade – probably the most common is to place first the name of the person whose application was received first. Job offers are made from the eligible list in the order the names appear on it. You will be notified of your grade and your rank as soon as all these computations have been made. This will be done as rapidly as possible.

People who are found to meet the requirements in the announcement are called "eligibles." Their names are put on a list of eligible candidates. An eligible's chances of getting a job depend on how high he stands on this list and how fast agencies are filling jobs from the list.

When a job is to be filled from a list of eligibles, the agency asks for the names of people on the list of eligibles for that job. When the civil service commission receives this request, it sends to the agency the names of the three people highest on this list. Or, if the job to be filled has specialized requirements, the office sends the agency the names of the top three persons who meet these requirements from the general list.

The appointing officer makes a choice from among the three people whose names were sent to him. If the selected person accepts the appointment, the names of the others are put back on the list to be considered for future openings.

That is the rule in hiring from all kinds of eligible lists, whether they are for typist, carpenter, chemist, or something else. For every vacancy, the appointing officer has his choice of any one of the top three eligibles on the list. This explains why the person whose name is on top of the list sometimes does not get an appointment when some of the persons lower on the list do. If the appointing officer chooses the second or third eligible, the No. 1 eligible does not get a job at once, but stays on the list until he is appointed or the list is terminated.

X. HOW TO PASS THE INTERVIEW TEST

The examination for which you applied requires an oral interview test. You have already taken the written test and you are now being called for the interview test – the final part of the formal examination.

You may think that it is not possible to prepare for an interview test and that there are no procedures to follow during an interview. Our purpose is to point out some things you can do in advance that will help you and some good rules to follow and pitfalls to avoid while you are being interviewed.

What is an interview supposed to test?

The written examination is designed to test the technical knowledge and competence of the candidate; the oral is designed to evaluate intangible qualities, not readily measured otherwise, and to establish a list showing the relative fitness of each candidate – as measured against his competitors – for the position sought. Scoring is not on the basis of "right" and "wrong," but on a sliding scale of values ranging from "not passable" to "outstanding." As a matter of fact, it is possible to achieve a relatively low score without a single "incorrect" answer because of evident weakness in the qualities being measured.

Occasionally, an examination may consist entirely of an oral test – either an individual or a group oral. In such cases, information is sought concerning the technical knowledges and abilities of the candidate, since there has been no written examination for this purpose. More commonly, however, an oral test is used to supplement a written examination.

Who conducts interviews?

The composition of oral boards varies among different jurisdictions. In nearly all, a representative of the personnel department serves as chairman. One of the members of the board may be a representative of the department in which the candidate would work. In some cases, "outside experts" are used, and, frequently, a businessman or some other representative of the general public is asked to serve. Labor and management or other special groups may be represented. The aim is to secure the services of experts in the appropriate field.

However the board is composed, it is a good idea (and not at all improper or unethical) to ascertain in advance of the interview who the members are and what groups they represent. When you are introduced to them, you will have some idea of their backgrounds and interests, and at least you will not stutter and stammer over their names.

What should be done before the interview?

While knowledge about the board members is useful and takes some of the surprise element out of the interview, there is other preparation which is more substantive. It *is* possible to prepare for an oral interview – in several ways:

1) Keep a copy of your application and review it carefully before the interview

This may be the only document before the oral board, and the starting point of the interview. Know what education and experience you have listed there, and the sequence and dates of all of it. Sometimes the board will ask you to review the highlights of your experience for them; you should not have to hem and haw doing it.

2) Study the class specification and the examination announcement

Usually, the oral board has one or both of these to guide them. The qualities, characteristics or knowledges required by the position sought are stated in these documents. They offer valuable clues as to the nature of the oral interview. For example, if the job involves supervisory responsibilities, the announcement will usually indicate that knowledge of modern supervisory methods and the qualifications of the candidate as a supervisor will be tested. If so, you can expect such questions, frequently in the form of a hypothetical situation which you are expected to solve. NEVER go into an oral without knowledge of the duties and responsibilities of the job you seek.

3) Think through each qualification required

Try to visualize the kind of questions you would ask if you were a board member. How well could you answer them? Try especially to appraise your own knowledge and background in each area, *measured against the job sought*, and identify any areas in which you are weak. Be critical and realistic – do not flatter yourself.

4) Do some general reading in areas in which you feel you may be weak

For example, if the job involves supervision and your past experience has NOT, some general reading in supervisory methods and practices, particularly in the field of human relations, might be useful. Do NOT study agency procedures or detailed manuals. The oral board will be testing your understanding and capacity, not your memory.

5) Get a good night's sleep and watch your general health and mental attitude

You will want a clear head at the interview. Take care of a cold or any other minor ailment, and of course, no hangovers.

What should be done on the day of the interview?

Now comes the day of the interview itself. Give yourself plenty of time to get there. Plan to arrive somewhat ahead of the scheduled time, particularly if your appointment is in the fore part of the day. If a previous candidate fails to appear, the board might be ready for you a bit early. By early afternoon an oral board is almost invariably behind schedule if there are many candidates, and you may have to wait. Take along a book or magazine to read, or your application to review, but leave any extraneous material in the waiting room when you go in for your interview. In any event, relax and compose yourself.

The matter of dress is important. The board is forming impressions about you – from your experience, your manners, your attitude, and your appearance. Give your personal appearance careful attention. Dress your best, but not your flashiest. Choose conservative, appropriate clothing, and be sure it is immaculate. This is a business interview, and your appearance should indicate that you regard it as such. Besides, being well groomed and properly dressed will help boost your confidence.

Sooner or later, someone will call your name and escort you into the interview room. *This is it.* From here on you are on your own. It is too late for any more preparation. But remember, you asked for this opportunity to prove your fitness, and you are here because your request was granted.

What happens when you go in?

The usual sequence of events will be as follows: The clerk (who is often the board stenographer) will introduce you to the chairman of the oral board, who will introduce you to the other members of the board. Acknowledge the introductions before you sit down. Do not be surprised if you find a microphone facing you or a stenotypist sitting by. Oral interviews are usually recorded in the event of an appeal or other review.

Usually the chairman of the board will open the interview by reviewing the highlights of your education and work experience from your application – primarily for the benefit of the other members of the board, as well as to get the material into the record. Do not interrupt or comment unless there is an error or significant misinterpretation; if that is the case, do not hesitate. But do not quibble about insignificant matters. Also, he will usually ask you some question about your education, experience or your present job – partly to get you to start talking and to establish the interviewing "rapport." He may start the actual questioning, or turn it over to one of the other members. Frequently, each member undertakes the questioning on a particular area, one in which he is perhaps most competent, so you can expect each member to participate in the examination. Because time is limited, you may also expect some rather abrupt switches in the direction the questioning takes, so do not be upset by it. Normally, a board member will not pursue a single line of questioning unless he discovers a particular strength or weakness.

After each member has participated, the chairman will usually ask whether any member has any further questions, then will ask you if you have anything you wish to add. Unless you are expecting this question, it may floor you. Worse, it may start you off on an extended, extemporaneous speech. The board is not usually seeking more information. The question is principally to offer you a last opportunity to present further qualifications or to indicate that you have nothing to add. So, if you feel that a significant qualification or characteristic has been overlooked, it is proper to point it out in a sentence or so. Do not compliment the board on the thoroughness of their examination – they have been sketchy, and you know it. If you wish, merely say, "No thank you, I have nothing further to add." This is a point where you can "talk yourself out" of a good impression or fail to present an important bit of information. Remember, *you close the interview yourself*.

The chairman will then say, "That is all, Mr. _____, thank you." Do not be startled; the interview is over, and quicker than you think. Thank him, gather your belongings and take your leave. Save your sigh of relief for the other side of the door.

How to put your best foot forward

Throughout this entire process, you may feel that the board individually and collectively is trying to pierce your defenses, seek out your hidden weaknesses and embarrass and confuse you. Actually, this is not true. They are obliged to make an appraisal of your qualifications for the job you are seeking, and they want to see you in your best light. Remember, they must interview all candidates and a non-cooperative candidate may become a failure in spite of their best efforts to bring out his qualifications. Here are 15 suggestions that will help you:

1) Be natural – Keep your attitude confident, not cocky

If you are not confident that you can do the job, do not expect the board to be. Do not apologize for your weaknesses, try to bring out your strong points. The board is interested in a positive, not negative, presentation. Cockiness will antagonize any board member and make him wonder if you are covering up a weakness by a false show of strength.

2) Get comfortable, but don't lounge or sprawl

Sit erectly but not stiffly. A careless posture may lead the board to conclude that you are careless in other things, or at least that you are not impressed by the importance of the occasion. Either conclusion is natural, even if incorrect. Do not fuss with your clothing, a pencil or an ashtray. Your hands may occasionally be useful to emphasize a point; do not let them become a point of distraction.

3) Do not wisecrack or make small talk

This is a serious situation, and your attitude should show that you consider it as such. Further, the time of the board is limited – they do not want to waste it, and neither should you.

4) Do not exaggerate your experience or abilities

In the first place, from information in the application or other interviews and sources, the board may know more about you than you think. Secondly, you probably will not get away with it. An experienced board is rather adept at spotting such a situation, so do not take the chance.

5) If you know a board member, do not make a point of it, yet do not hide it

Certainly you are not fooling him, and probably not the other members of the board. Do not try to take advantage of your acquaintanceship – it will probably do you little good.

6) Do not dominate the interview

Let the board do that. They will give you the clues – do not assume that you have to do all the talking. Realize that the board has a number of questions to ask you, and do not try to take up all the interview time by showing off your extensive knowledge of the answer to the first one.

7) Be attentive

You only have 20 minutes or so, and you should keep your attention at its sharpest throughout. When a member is addressing a problem or question to you, give him your undivided attention. Address your reply principally to him, but do not exclude the other board members.

8) Do not interrupt

A board member may be stating a problem for you to analyze. He will ask you a question when the time comes. Let him state the problem, and wait for the question.

9) Make sure you understand the question

Do not try to answer until you are sure what the question is. If it is not clear, restate it in your own words or ask the board member to clarify it for you. However, do not haggle about minor elements.

10) Reply promptly but not hastily

A common entry on oral board rating sheets is "candidate responded readily," or "candidate hesitated in replies." Respond as promptly and quickly as you can, but do not jump to a hasty, ill-considered answer.

11) Do not be peremptory in your answers

A brief answer is proper – but do not fire your answer back. That is a losing game from your point of view. The board member can probably ask questions much faster than you can answer them.

12) Do not try to create the answer you think the board member wants

He is interested in what kind of mind you have and how it works – not in playing games. Furthermore, he can usually spot this practice and will actually grade you down on it.

13) Do not switch sides in your reply merely to agree with a board member

Frequently, a member will take a contrary position merely to draw you out and to see if you are willing and able to defend your point of view. Do not start a debate, yet do not surrender a good position. If a position is worth taking, it is worth defending.

14) Do not be afraid to admit an error in judgment if you are shown to be wrong

The board knows that you are forced to reply without any opportunity for careful consideration. Your answer may be demonstrably wrong. If so, admit it and get on with the interview.

15) Do not dwell at length on your present job

The opening question may relate to your present assignment. Answer the question but do not go into an extended discussion. You are being examined for a *new* job, not your present one. As a matter of fact, try to phrase ALL your answers in terms of the job for which you are being examined.

Basis of Rating

Probably you will forget most of these "do's" and "don'ts" when you walk into the oral interview room. Even remembering them all will not ensure you a passing grade. Perhaps you did not have the qualifications in the first place. But remembering them will help you to put your best foot forward, without treading on the toes of the board members.

Rumor and popular opinion to the contrary notwithstanding, an oral board wants you to make the best appearance possible. They know you are under pressure – but they also want to see how you respond to it as a guide to what your reaction would be under the pressures of the job you seek. They will be influenced by the degree of poise you display, the personal traits you show and the manner in which you respond.

ABOUT THIS BOOK

This book contains tests divided into Examination Sections. Go through each test, answering every question in the margin. We have also attached a sample answer sheet at the back of the book that can be removed and used. At the end of each test look at the answer key and check your answers. On the ones you got wrong, look at the right answer choice and learn. Do not fill in the answers first. Do not memorize the questions and answers, but understand the answer and principles involved. On your test, the questions will likely be different from the samples. Questions are changed and new ones added. If you understand these past questions you should have success with any changes that arise. Tests may consist of several types of questions. We have additional books on each subject should more study be advisable or necessary for you. Finally, the more you study, the better prepared you will be. This book is intended to be the last thing you study before you walk into the examination room. Prior study of relevant texts is also recommended. NLC publishes some of these in our Fundamental Series. Knowledge and good sense are important factors in passing your exam. Good luck also helps. So now study this Passbook, absorb the material contained within and take that knowledge into the examination. Then do your best to pass that exam.

EXAMINATION SECTION

EXAMINATION SECTION
TEST 1

DIRECTIONS: Each question or incomplete statement is followed by several suggested answers or completions. Select the one that BEST answers the question or completes the statement. *PRINT THE LETTER OF THE CORRECT ANSWER IN THE SPACE AT THE RIGHT.*

1. There are a considerable number of forms and reports to be submitted on schedule by a building custodian.
   The ADVISABLE method of accomplishing this duty is to

   A. fill out the reports at odd times during the days when you have free time
   B. schedule a definite period of the work week for completing these forms and reports
   C. assign your foreman or cleaner to handle all these forms for you and to have them available on time
   D. classify or group the forms and reports and fill out only one of each group and refer the other forms or reports to the ones completed

2. In enforcing compliance with safety regulations, you should take the attitude that they must be complied with because

   A. every accident can be prevented
   B. safety regulations are based on reason and experience with the best methods of accident prevention
   C. compliance with safety regulations will make other safety efforts unnecessary
   D. they are the law, and law enforcement is an end in itself

3. The use of trisodium phosphate in cleaning marble should be avoided because

   A. it discolors the surface of the marble
   B. the salt crystals get in the pores, expand, and crack the marble
   C. it pits the glazed surface and bleaches the marble
   D. it builds up a slick surface on the marble

4. The use of a concentrated cleaning solution on painted or varnished woodwork

   A. results in burning the pigments of paint or varnish, causing dull, streaky surfaces
   B. cuts down on time and energy in maintaining clean, unblemished surfaces
   C. insures spotless, clean, bright surfaces
   D. is detrimental to the health of the cleaners

5. A building custodian will make the BEST impression on the office staff if he

   A. impresses them with the importance of his job
   B. says little and is cold and distant
   C. is easy-going and good-natured
   D. is courteous and performs his duties with as little delay as possible

6. Domestic hot water storage reservoirs should be thoroughly cleaned once

   A. a week   B. a month
   C. a year   D. every two years

7. A *pH* value of 4 would indicate a(n)

   A. acid solution
   B. neutral solution
   C. alkaline solution
   D. low pressure heating system

8. When the diaphragm or bellows of a thermostatic radiator trap is found to be dirty, it is USUALLY cleaned with

   A. turpentine
   B. carbon tetrachloride
   C. kerosene
   D. mild soap and water

9. The CHIEF purpose of a plumbing trap is to

   A. permit air to enter the sewer
   B. prevent the entrance of sewer gas into the building
   C. break the shock of the water draining off
   D. siphon off the waste water

10. The safety device on the gas pilot flame of a gas-fired apparatus should operate on pilot flame failure to

    A. bypass the main gas supply directly to the flue
    B. switch over to auxiliary bottled gas pilot flame
    C. shut off the gas supply
    D. introduce sufficient excess air to keep the furnace below the lower explosive limit

11. When instructing employees in regard to their duties in case of fire, a supervisor should

    A. tell employees to take no action until the fire department equipment has arrived
    B. tell all employees to go to the scene of the fire
    C. assign each employee specific duties
    D. tell employees to extinguish the fire before calling the supervisor or the fire department

12. The PRINCIPAL value of a good report is that it

    A. is always available for reference
    B. impresses department heads with the need for immediate action
    C. reflects upon the writer of the report
    D. expedites official business

13. The quality of work performed by personnel engaged in building cleaning is BEST evaluated by

    A. studying building cleaning expenditures
    B. studying time records of personnel
    C. analyzing complaints by building occupants
    D. inspecting the building periodically

14. Of the following, a building custodian need NOT be kept informed on

    A. departmental management policies
    B. terms of union contracts covering his subordinates
    C. developments of current interest in custodial operations
    D. current rate of interest on municipal bonds

15. The BEST way to make work assignments to persons required to clean a multi-story building is to

    A. allow the persons to pick their room or area assignments out of a hat
    B. make specific room or area assignments to each person separately
    C. rotate room and area assignments daily according to a chart posted on the bulletin board
    D. each week let a different member of the group make the room or area assignment

16. One important use of accident reports is to provide information that may be used to reduce the possibility of similar accidents.
    The MOST valuable entry on the report for this purpose is the

    A. name of the victim
    B. injury sustained by the victim
    C. cause of the accident
    D. location of the accident

17. Suppose that an emergency has arisen which requires you to cancel some of the jobs scheduled for that day.
    Of the following jobs, the one that can be eliminated for that day with LEAST effect on the proper operation and maintenance of the building is

    A. mopping and cleaning toilet rooms
    B. checking public stairs and corridors for hazards
    C. improving the location of supplies in the storeroom
    D. replacing broken window panes in offices

18. Of the following, a building custodian's attitude toward grievances should be to

    A. pay little attention to little grievances
    B. be very alert to grievances and make adjustments in existing conditions to appease all of them
    C. know the most frequent causes of grievances and strive to prevent them from arising
    D. maintain rigid discipline of a nature that *smoothes out* all grievances

19. A heavy snowfall must be removed from the sidewalks around the building. You, as building custodian, have assigned two men to shovel snow from the walks. After an interval, you check and find they are bickering as to how much each is shoveling, and no snow is being removed.
    In this situation, you should

    A. stand with them to supervise the snow removal and to be sure the work is divided evenly
    B. assign two other men to snow removal and send the original two back to their usual chores
    C. put the man with seniority in full charge of the other man
    D. separate the men by sending them to opposite ends of the walks to shovel alone, with a warning that you will be checking on their progress at short intervals

20. Of the following, safety on the job is BEST assured by 20.____

    A. keeping alert
    B. following every rule
    C. working very slowly
    D. never working alone

KEY (CORRECT ANSWERS)

1.	B	11.	C
2.	B	12.	D
3.	B	13.	D
4.	A	14.	D
5.	D	15.	B
6.	C	16.	C
7.	A	17.	C
8.	C	18.	C
9.	B	19.	D
10.	C	20.	A

TEST 2

DIRECTIONS: Each question or incomplete statement is followed by several suggested answers or completions. Select the one that BEST answers the question or completes the statement. *PRINT THE LETTER OF THE CORRECT ANSWER IN THE SPACE AT THE RIGHT.*

1. A foam-type fire extinguisher extinguishes fires by 1._____

    A. cooling *only*
    B. drenching *only*
    C. smothering *only*
    D. cooling and smothering

2. The extinguishing agent in a soda-acid fire extinguisher is 2._____

    A. carbon dioxide
    B. water
    C. carbon tetrachloride
    D. calcium chloride solution

3. The PROPER extinguisher to use on an electrical fire in an operating electric motor is 3._____

    A. foam
    B. carbon dioxide
    C. soda and acid
    D. water

4. When an extension ladder is in place and ready to be used, the rope used to extend the ladder should be 4._____

    A. left hanging free out of the way of the climber's feet
    B. used to raise and lower tools to the man on the ladder
    C. used as a means of steadying the climber
    D. tied securely around a lower rung

5. The PRINCIPAL characteristic of panic locks or bolts on doors of places of public assembly is that they 5._____

    A. allow the doors to open outwardly with sufficient pressure on the bars of the lock
    B. allow the doors to open inwardly with sufficient pressure on the bars of the lock
    C. prevent the door from opening under impact load
    D. may be opened with any tumbler lock key

6. The MAIN purpose of periodic inspections and tests of electrical equipment is to 6._____

    A. encourage the men to take better care of the equipment
    B. make the men familiar with the equipment
    C. discover minor faults before they develop into major faults
    D. keep the men busy during otherwise slack periods

7. Standard, extra strong, and double extra strong welded steel pipe of a given size all have the SAME 7._____

    A. outside diameter
    B. inside diameter
    C. average diameter
    D. flow capacity for any given flow velocity

8. In reference to domestic gas piping,

   A. couplings with running threads are used to join pipes
   B. risers must have a drip leg and cap at bottom
   C. gasketed unions may be used in joining pipe
   D. composition disc globe valves are used to throttle the gas

9. Chewing gum should be removed from rubber, asphalt, or linoleum flooring with

   A. a putty knife
   B. steel wool
   C. gritty compounds
   D. a solvent

10. Which one of the following is the BEST procedure to follow when the linoleum floor of a meeting room containing movable furniture is to be mopped?

    A. The furniture should be moved by sliding it along the floor to prevent injury to the cleaners.
    B. The furniture should not be moved.
    C. The furniture should be moved by lifting it and carrying it to a clear spot to prevent damage to the linoleum.
    D. Very little water should be used in order to prevent the legs of the furniture from getting wet.

11. Asphalt tile flooring that has been subjected to oily compounds

    A. may last indefinitely
    B. must be removed and replaced with new asphalt tile immediately
    C. may be restored to hardness and lustre by several moppings with hot water and several applications of water wax
    D. must be restored to original condition by several moppings with kerosene

12. The use of alcohol in water for washing windows is NOT recommended because it

    A. is a hazard to the cleaner in that he may be affected by the fumes
    B. will damage the paint around the edges of the glass
    C. pits the surface of the glass
    D. destroys the bristles of the brush applying the solution to the pane

13. Of the following, the BEST material to use for removing grass stains on marble or wood is

    A. oxalic acid
    B. chloride of lime
    C. sodium silicate
    D. sodium hypochlorite

14. Shades or Venetian blinds are PREFERABLY cleaned with a

    A. feather duster
    B. counter brush
    C. damp sponge
    D. vacuum cleaner

15. Asphalt tile floors are PREFERABLY polished with

    A. water emulsion wax
    B. wax in solution with benzol
    C. a high fatty acid soap
    D. sodium metaphosphate

16. Washing soda is used to

    A. eliminate the need for rinse mopping or wiping
    B. make the cleaning compound abrasive
    C. decrease the wetting power of water
    D. increase the wetting power of water

17. Varnish or lacquer may be used as a sealer on floors finished with

    A. asphalt tiles
    B. linoleum
    C. rubber tiles
    D. cork tiles

18. A long-handled deck scrub brush is MOST effective when scrubbing

    A. large open areas
    B. stair treads
    C. small flat areas
    D. long corridors

19. The BEST method for preventing the infestation of a building by rats is to

    A. use cats
    B. use rat traps
    C. eliminate rat harborages in the building
    D. use poisoned bait

20. The one of the following foodstuffs which, if allowed to remain on ordinary asphalt tile, will MOST likely be most injurious to it is

    A. milk
    B. maple syrup
    C. ketchup
    D. salad oil

KEY (CORRECT ANSWERS)

1.	D	11.	C
2.	B	12.	B
3.	B	13.	D
4.	D	14.	D
5.	A	15.	A
6.	C	16.	D
7.	A	17.	D
8.	B	18.	C
9.	A	19.	C
10.	C	20.	D

TEST 3

DIRECTIONS: Each question or incomplete statement is followed by several suggested answers or completions. Select the one that BEST answers the question or completes the statement. *PRINT THE LETTER OF THE CORRECT ANSWER IN THE SPACE AT THE RIGHT.*

1. Employees engaged in cleaning operations who are issued rubber gloves to protect their hands against caustic solutions should be warned that   1._____

    A. such solution allowed to spill over the glove top into the space between the glove and the hand may damage the skin of the hand
    B. rubber gloves have a very short life in contact with caustic solutions
    C. harmful gases can penetrate the rubber and harm even dry hands
    D. contact of the hands with glove-type rubber for over an hour is harmful

2. Pyrethrins are used as   2._____

    A. insecticides
    B. germicides
    C. waxes
    D. detergents

3. Water hammer is   3._____

    A. a special hammer used to remove scale from a radiator
    B. caused by water in steam lines
    C. caused by excessive boiler pressure
    D. caused by low water level in the boiler

4. Which of the following is USUALLY used in the construction of a steam pressure gauge?   4._____

    A. Perfect circle tube
    B. Venturi tube
    C. Bourdon tube
    D. Elastic linkage

5. Usually when a large room is gradually filled with people, the room temperature   5._____

    A. and humidity both decrease
    B. increases and the humidity decreases
    C. and humidity increase
    D. decreases and humidity increases

6. A foot valve at the intake end of the suction line of a pump serves MAINLY to   6._____

    A. maintain pump prime
    B. filter out large particles in the fluid
    C. increase the maximum suction lift of the pump
    D. increase pump flow rate

7. A pressure gauge attached to a standpipe system shows a pressure of 36 pounds per sq. in.
The head of water, in feet, above the gauge is MOST NEARLY   7._____

    A. 24
    B. 36
    C. 60
    D. 83

8. Of the following, the term *vapor barrier* would MOST likely be associated with

   A. electric service installation
   B. insulation materials
   C. fuel oil tank installation
   D. domestic gas piping

9. Pitot tubes are used to

   A. test feed water for impurities
   B. measure air or gas flow in a duct
   C. prevent overheating of elements of a steam gauge
   D. control the ignition system of an oil burner

10. In warm air heating and in ventilating systems, laboratories and kitchens should NOT be equipped with return ducts in order to

    A. keep air velocities in other returns as high as possible
    B. reduce fire hazards
    C. reduce the possibility of circulating odors through the system
    D. keep the temperature high in these rooms

11. One square foot of equivalent direct steam radiation (EDR) is equivalent to a heat emission of _____ BTU per _____.

    A. 150; hour
    B. 240; minute
    C. 150; minute
    D. 240; hour

12. Of the following, the one which is LEAST likely to cause continuous vibration of an operating motor is

    A. a faulty starting circuit
    B. excessive belt tension
    C. the misalignment of motor and driven equipment
    D. loose bearings

13. The function of a steam trap is to

    A. remove sediment and dirt from steam
    B. remove air and non-condensible gases from steam
    C. relieve excessive steam pressure to the atmosphere
    D. remove condensate from a pipe or an apparatus

14. The temperature at which air is just saturated with the moisture present in it is called its

    A. relative humidity
    B. absolute humidity
    C. humid temperature
    D. dew point

15. If scale forms on the seat of a float-operated boiler feed water regulator, the MOST likely result is

    A. internal corrosion of the boiler shell
    B. insufficient supply of water to the boiler
    C. flooding of the boiler
    D. shutting down of the oil burner by the low water cut-out

16. The compound gauge in the oil suction line shows a high vacuum. This is USUALLY an indication of

    A. a dirty oil strainer
    B. low oil level in the fuel oil storage tank
    C. a leak in the fuel oil preheater
    D. an obstruction in the fuel oil preheater

17. Of the following, the information which is LEAST important on a boiler room log sheet is the

    A. stack temperature readings
    B. CO_2 readings
    C. number of boilers in operation
    D. boiler room humidity

18. Pitting and corrosion of the water side of the boiler heating surfaces is due MAINLY to the boiler water containing dissolved

    A. oxygen
    B. hydrogen
    C. soda-ash
    D. sodium sulphite

19. The combustion efficiency of a boiler can be determined with a CO_2

    A. flue gas temperature
    B. boiler room humidity
    C. outside air temperature
    D. under fire draft

20. The try-cocks of steam boilers are used to

    A. find the height of water in the boiler
    B. test steam pressure in the boiler
    C. empty the boiler of water
    D. act as safety valves

KEY (CORRECT ANSWERS)

1.	A	11.	D
2.	A	12.	A
3.	B	13.	D
4.	C	14.	D
5.	C	15.	C
6.	A	16.	A
7.	D	17.	D
8.	B	18.	A
9.	B	19.	A
10.	C	20.	A

TEST 4

DIRECTIONS: Each question or incomplete statement is followed by several suggested answers or completions. Select the one that BEST answers the question or completes the statement. *PRINT THE LETTER OF THE CORRECT ANSWER IN THE SPACE AT THE RIGHT.*

1. The reason for sweating inside a refrigerator cabinet is 1._____

    A. high percent running time of compressor unit
    B. high cabinet air temperature
    C. defective expansion valve
    D. a poor door seal

2. Of the following ingredients, the ones to be mixed with water to *point-up* the brickwork of a building are: 1 part cement, 2._____

    A. 2 parts sand, 3 parts gravel
    B. 3 parts sand, 4 parts gravel
    C. 3 parts sand
    D. 5 parts sand

3. Acid soils can BEST be neutralized by liberal applications of 3._____

    A. manure   B. salt
    C. lime   D. powdered-basalt

4. Summer blooming flower bulbs should be stored in a _____ place. 4._____

    A. warm, dry   B. warm, moist
    C. cool, moist   D. cool, dry

5. A certain 31-day month had an average temperature of 45 Fahrenheit. The number of degree days for this month is 5._____

    A. 31   B. 450   C. 620   D. 1395

6. While concrete is *curing*, it is MOST desirable to 6._____

    A. expose the concrete to sun and air as much as possible
    B. keep the concrete surface moist
    C. maintain a temperature of not more than 60°F
    D. maintain a temperature of at least 80°F

7. To join two lengths of pipe together in a solid straight run, the fitting to use is a 7._____

    A. coupling   B. tee
    C. hickey   D. shoulder nipple

8. New copper flashing that has been soldered should be 8._____

    A. muriatic acid   B. plain water
    C. benzine   D. washing soda or lye

11

9. The intercooler of a two-stage air compressor is connected to the compressor between the

   A. two stages
   B. filter and the first stage
   C. second stage and the receiver
   D. receiver and point of usage of the air

10. Both terms *tank* and *close* apply USUALLY to

    A. electric generator couplings
    B. freon storage units
    C. pipe nipples
    D. ventilation plenum chambers

11. The commercial fertilizer *5-10-5* refers to

    A. 5% nitrogen, 10% phosphoric acid, 5% potash
    B. 5% rotted manure, 10% calcium chloride, 5% bone meal
    C. 5% soda, 10% tobacco dust, 5% bone meal
    D. 5% tobacco dust, 10% rotted manure, 5% sulphur

12. The slope or slant of a soil line is 1/4" per foot. If this drainage line is 50' long, the difference in elevation from one end to the other is, in feet, MOST NEARLY

    A. 0.55   B. 1.04   C. 2.08   D. 12.5

13. Oil is used with sharpening stones when sharpening wood chisels in order to

    A. reduce the effort needed to move the blade over the stone
    B. maintain the oil temper of the steel used for the chisel
    C. flush off the small metal chips and clear the cutting edges of the abrasive grit
    D. reduce the temperature due to friction

14. A maintenance man checking a refrigerator for a freon leak would use a

    A. soap and water solution
    B. halide torch
    C. glycerine solution
    D. linseed oil and whiting solution

15. A basement floor area of 5000 square feet is under 9 inches of water.
    If this 9 inches of water is to be pumped out of the basement in one hour, the required capacity of the portable pump, in gallons per minute, is MOST NEARLY

    A. 63   B. 470   C. 1020   D. 2810

16. A MAJOR advantage of keeping a perpetual inventory of supplies is that it

    A. gives a current record of the supplies available at all times
    B. reduces the work required to distribute supplies
    C. avoids the need for periodic physical inventories
    D. shows who is using excessive supplies

17. Employees generally do NOT object to strict rules and regulations if they   17.____

    A. are enforced without bias or favor
    B. result in more material gain
    C. deal with relatively unimportant phases of the work
    D. affect the supervisors more than their subordinates

18. In order to have building employees willing to follow standardized cleaning and mainte-   18.____
    nance procedures, the supervisor MUST be prepared to

    A. work alongside the employees
    B. demonstrate the reasonableness of the procedures
    C. offer incentive pay for their use
    D. be adamant in opposing changes in the standardized procedures

19. Of the following, the MOST important step when accepting incoming shipments of stan-   19.____
    dard items normally carried in stock is to check the items for

    A. electrical performance   B. chemical composition
    C. quantity delivered   D. mechanical performance

20. The orderly arrangement of supplies in storage USUALLY   20.____

    A. takes too much time to be worthwhile
    B. is important only in large warehouses
    C. is essential for stock selection and inventory purposes
    D. cannot be accomplished when package sizes vary

KEY (CORRECT ANSWERS)

1.	D	11.	A
2.	C	12.	B
3.	C	13.	C
4.	D	14.	B
5.	C	15.	B
6.	B	16.	A
7.	A	17.	A
8.	D	18.	B
9.	A	19.	C
10.	C	20.	C

EXAMINATION SECTION
TEST 1

DIRECTIONS: Each question or incomplete statement is followed by several suggested answers or completions. Select the one that BEST answers the question or completes the statement. *PRINT THE LETTER OF THE CORRECT ANSWER IN THE SPACE AT THE RIGHT.*

1. Before starting any lawn mowing, the distance between the blade and a flat surface should be measured with a ruler. This distance should be such that the cut of the grass above the ground is _____ inch(es).   1._____

    A. 1   B. 1 1/2   C. 2   D. 3

2. Strainers in a number 6 fuel oil system should be checked once a   2._____

    A. day   B. week   C. month   D. year

3. The spinning cup on a rotary cup oil burner should be cleaned once   3._____

    A. a day
    B. a week
    C. every two weeks
    D. a month

4. Terrazzo floors should be cleaned daily with a   4._____

    A. damp mop using clear water
    B. damp mop using a strong alkaline solution
    C. damp mop using a mild acid solution
    D. dust mop treated with vegetable oil

5. New installations of vinyl-asbestos floors should   5._____

    A. never be machine scrubbed
    B. be dry-buffed weekly
    C. be swept daily, using an oily compound
    D. never be swept with treated dust mops

6. Standpipe fire hose shall be inspected   6._____

    A. monthly
    B. quarterly
    C. semi-annually
    D. annually

7. All portable fire extinguishers shall be inspected once   7._____

    A. a year
    B. a month
    C. a week
    D. every 3 months

8. Soda-acid and foam-type fire extinguishers shall be discharged and recharged at least once   8._____

    A. each year
    B. every two years
    C. every six months
    D. each month

9. Elevator *safeties* under the car shall be tested once each   9._____

    A. day   B. week   C. month   D. quarter

10. Key-type fire alarms in public school buildings shall be tested

    A. daily
    B. weekly
    C. monthly
    D. quarterly

11. Combustion efficiency can be determined from an appropriate chart used in conjunction with _____ temperature and

    A. steam; steam pressure
    B. flue gas; percentage of CO_2
    C. flue gas; fuel heating value
    D. oil; steam pressure

12. In the combustion of common fuels, the major boiler heat loss is due to

    A. incomplete combustion
    B. moisture in the fuel
    C. heat radiation
    D. heat lost in the flue gases

13. The MOST important reason for blowing down a boiler water column and gauge glass is to

    A. prevent the gauge glass level from rising too high
    B. relieve stresses in the gauge glass
    C. insure a true water level reading
    D. insure a true pressure gauge reading

14. The secondary voltage of a transformer used for ignition in a fuel oil burner has a range of MOST NEARLY _____ volts to _____ volts.

    A. 120; 240
    B. 440; 660
    C. 660; 1,200
    D. 5,000; 15,000

15. Assume that during the month of April there were 3 days with an average outdoor temperature of 30° F, 7 days with 40° F, 10 days with 50° F, 3 days with 60° F, and 7 days with 65° F.
    The number of degree days for the month was

    A. 330   B. 445   C. 595   D. 1,150

16. The pH of boiler feedwater is usually maintained within the range of

    A. 4 to 5   B. 6 to 7   C. 10 to 12   D. 13 to 14

17. The admission of steam to the coils of a domestic hot water supply tank is regulated by a(n)

    A. pressure regulating valve
    B. immersion type temperature gauge
    C. check valve
    D. thermostatic control valve

18. The device which senses primary air failure in a rotary cup oil burner is usually called a(n)

    A. vaporstat
    B. anemometer
    C. venturi
    D. pressure gauge

19. The device which starts and stops the flow of oil into an automatic rotary cup oil burner is usually called a(n) _____ valve.

    A. magnetic oil
    B. oil metering
    C. oil check
    D. relief

20. A vacuum breaker, used on a steam heated domestic hot water tank, is usually connected to the

    A. circulating pump
    B. tank wall
    C. aquastat
    D. steam coil flange

21. A vacuum pump in a low pressure steam heating system which is equipped with a float switch, a vacuum switch, a magnetic starter, and a selector switch can be operated on

    A. float, vacuum, or automatic
    B. float, vacuum, or continuous
    C. vacuum, automatic, or continuous
    D. float, automatic, or continuous

22. If the temperature of the condensate returning to the vacuum pump in a low pressure steam vacuum heating system is above 180° F, the trouble may be caused by

    A. faulty radiator traps
    B. room thermostats being set too high
    C. uninsulated return lines
    D. too many radiators being shut off

23. A feedwater regulator operates to

    A. shut down the burner when the water is low
    B. maintain the water in the boiler at a predetermined level
    C. drain the water from the boiler
    D. regulate the temperature of the feedwater

24. An automatically fired steam boiler is equipped with an automatic low water cut-off. The low water cut-off is usually actuated by

    A. steam pressure
    B. fuel pressure
    C. float action
    D. water temperature

25. Low pressure steam or an electric heater is usually required for heating No. _____ fuel oil.

    A. 1 B. 2 C. 4 D. 6

KEY (CORRECT ANSWERS)

1.	C	11.	B
2.	A	12.	D
3.	A	13.	C
4.	A	14.	D
5.	B	15.	B
6.	B	16.	C
7.	B	17.	D
8.	A	18.	A
9.	C	19.	A
10.	A	20.	D

21.	D
22.	A
23.	B
24.	C
25.	D

TEST 2

DIRECTIONS: Each question or incomplete statement is followed by several suggested answers or completions. Select the one that BEST answers the question or completes the statement. *PRINT THE LETTER OF THE CORRECT ANSWER IN THE SPACE AT THE RIGHT.*

1. A compound gauge is calibrated to read   1.____

   A. pressure only
   B. vacuum only
   C. vacuum and pressure
   D. temperature and humidity

2. In a mechanical pressure-atomizing type oil burner, the oil is atomized by using an atomizing tip and   2.____

   A. steam pressure
   B. pump pressure
   C. compressed air
   D. a spinning cup

3. A good over-the-fire draft in a natural draft furnace should be approximately _____ inches of water _____.   3.____

   A. 5.0; positive pressure
   B. 0.05; positive pressure
   C. 0.05; vacuum
   D. 5.0; vacuum

4. When it is necessary to add chemicals to a heating boiler, it should be done   4.____

   A. immediately after boiler blowdown
   B. after the boiler has been cleaned internally of sludge, scale, and other foreign matter
   C. at periods when condensate flow to the boiler is small
   D. at a time when there is a heavy flow of condensate to the boiler

5. The modutrol motor on a rotary cup oil burner burning #6 fuel oil automatically operates the primary air damper,   5.____

   A. secondary air damper, and oil metering valve
   B. secondary air damper, and magnetic oil valve
   C. oil metering valve, and magnetic oil valve
   D. and magnetic oil valve

6. The manual-reset pressuretrol is classified as a _____ Control.   6.____

   A. Safety and Operating
   B. Limit and Operating
   C. Limit and Safety
   D. Limit, Operating, and Safety

7. Sodium sulphite is added to boiler feedwater to   7.____

   A. avoid caustic embrittlement
   B. increase the pH value
   C. reduce the tendency of foaming in the steam drum
   D. remove dissolved oxygen

8. Neat cement is a mixture of cement,

   A. putty, and water
   B. and water
   C. lime and water
   D. salt, and water

9. In a concrete mix of 1:2:4, the 2 refers to the amount of

   A. sand   B. cement   C. stone   D. water

10. The word *natatorium* means MOST NEARLY a(n)

    A. auditorium
    B. playroom
    C. gymnasium
    D. indoor swimming pool

11. Plated metal surfaces which are protected by a thin coat of clear lacquer should be cleaned with a(n)

    A. abrasive compound
    B. liquid polish
    C. mild soap solution
    D. lemon oil solution

12. Wet mop filler replacements are ordered by

    A. length
    B. weight
    C. number of strands
    D. trade number

13. The BEST way to determine the value of a cleaning material is by

    A. performance testing
    B. manufacturer's literature
    C. written specifications
    D. interviews with manufacturer's salesman

14. The instructions on a container of cleaning compound states, *Mix one pound of compound in 5 gallons of water.* Using these instructions, the amount of compound which should be added to 15 quarts of water is MOST likely _____ ounces.

    A. 3   B. 8   C. 12   D. 48

15. The MOST usual cause of paint blisters is

    A. too much oil in the paint
    B. moisture under the paint coat
    C. a heavy coat of paint
    D. improper drying of the paint

16. The floor that should NOT be machined scrubbed is a(n)

    A. lobby
    B. lunchroom
    C. gymnasium
    D. auditorium aisle

17. Pick-up sweeping in a school building is the occasional removal of the more conspicuous loose dirt from corridors and lobbies.
    This type of sweeping should be done

    A. after scrubbing or waxing of floors
    B. with the aid of a sweeping compound
    C. at night after school hours
    D. during regular school hours

18. According to recommended practice, when a steam boiler is taken out of service for a long period of time, the boiler drums should FIRST be

    A. drained completely while the water is hot (above 212° F)
    B. drained completely after the water has been cooled down to 180° F
    C. filled completely without draining
    D. filled to the level of the top try cock

19. Specifications concerning window cleaners' anchors and safety belts must be in compliance with the rules and regulations outlined in the

    A. State Labor Law and Board of Standards and Appeals
    B. Building Code
    C. Fire Department Safety Manual
    D. National Protection Association

20. If it is not possible to plant new shrubs immediately upon delivery in the spring, they should be stored in a(n)

    A. sheltered outdoor area   B. unsheltered outdoor area
    C. boiler room   D. warm place indoors

21. Peat moss is generally used for its

    A. food value   B. nitrogen
    C. alkalinity   D. moisture retaining quality

22. The legal minimum age of employees engaged for cleaning windows in the state is _____ years.

    A. 16   B. 17   C. 18   D. 21

23. Pruning of street trees is the responsibility of the

    A. School Custodian Engineer
    B. Board of Education
    C. Department of Parks
    D. Borough President's Office

24. The prevention and control of vermin and rodents in a school building is PRIMARILY a matter of

    A. maintaining good housekeeping on a continuous basis
    B. periodic use of an exterminator's service
    C. calling in the exterminator when necessary
    D. cleaning the building thoroughly during school vacation

25. The MAIN classification of lumber used for construction purposes is known as _____ lumber.

    A. industrial   B. commercial
    C. finish   D. yard

KEY (CORRECT ANSWERS)

1.	C	11.	C
2.	B	12.	B
3.	C	13.	A
4.	D	14.	C
5.	A	15.	B
6.	C	16.	C
7.	D	17.	D
8.	B	18.	B
9.	A	19.	A
10.	D	20.	A

21. D
22. C
23. C
24. A
25. D

TEST 3

DIRECTIONS: Each question or incomplete statement is followed by several suggested answers or completions. Select the one that BEST answers the question or completes the statement. *PRINT THE LETTER OF THE CORRECT ANSWER IN THE SPACE AT THE RIGHT.*

1. Oil-soaked waste and rags should be

    A. deposited in a self-closing metal can
    B. piled in the open
    C. stored in the supply closet
    D. rolled up and be available for the next job

1.____

2. Inspection for safety should be included as part of the custodian engineer's _____ inspection.

    A. daily   B. weekly   C. monthly   D. quarterly

2.____

3. Of the following classifications, the one which pertains to fires in electrical equipment is Class

    A. A   B. B   C. C   D. D

3.____

4. The type of portable fire extinguisher which is PARTICULARLY suited for extinguishing flammable liquid fires is the _____ type.

    A. soda-acid   B. foam
    C. pump tank   D. loaded stream

4.____

5. Of the following liquids, the one which has the LOWEST flash point is

    A. kerosene   B. gasoline
    C. benzene   D. carbon tetrachloride

5.____

6. When giving first aid to an injured person, which one of the following should you NOT do?

    A. Administer medication internally
    B. Send for a physician
    C. Control bleeding
    D. Treat for shock

6.____

7. In reference to firefighting, fires are of such complexity that

    A. no plans or methods of attack can be formulated in advance
    B. the problem must be considered in advance and methods of attack formulated
    C. an appointed committee is necessary to direct fighting at the fire
    D. no planned procedures can be relied on

7.____

8. The heat of a soldering copper should be tested

    A. with solder
    B. by holding it near kraft paper
    C. by holding it near your hand
    D. with water

8.____

23

9. Safety on the job is BEST assured by

   A. keeping alert
   B. following every rule
   C. working very slowly
   D. never working alone

10. One important use of accident reports is to provide information that may be used to reduce the possibility of similar accidents.
    The MOST valuable entry on the report for this purpose is the

    A. time lost due to accident
    B. date of the occurrence
    C. injury sustained by the victim
    D. cause of the accident

11. If the directions given by your superior are NOT clear, the BEST thing for you to do is to

    A. ask to have the directions repeated and clarified
    B. proceed to do the work taking a chance on doing the right thing
    C. do nothing until some later time when you can find out exactly what is wanted
    D. ask one of the other men in your crew what he would do under the circumstances

12. Of the following procedures concerning grievances of subordinate personnel, the custodian engineer should maintain an attitude of

    A. paying little attention to little grievances
    B. being very alert to grievances and make adjustments in existing conditions to appease all personnel
    C. knowing the most frequent causes of grievances and strive to prevent them from arising
    D. maintaining rigid discipline of a nature that *smooths out* all grievances

13. Of the following, the BEST course of action to take to settle a dispute or conflict between two employees is to

    A. insist that the two employees settle the case between themselves
    B. call in each one separately and after hearing their cases presented, decide the issue
    C. bring both in for a conference at the same time and make the decision in their presence
    D. have both present their points of view and arguments in a written memoranda and on this basis make your decision

14. If, as a custodian engineer, you discover an error in your report submitted to the main office, you should

    A. do nothing, since it is possible that one error will have little effect on the total report
    B. wait until the error is discovered in the main office and then offer to work overtime to correct it
    C. go directly to the supervisor in the main office after working hours and ask him unofficially to correct the error
    D. notify the main office immediately so that the error can be corrected, if necessary

15. There are a considerable number of forms and reports to be submitted on schedule by the custodian engineer. The advisable method of accomplishing this duty is to

    A. fill out the reports at odd times during the days when you have free time
    B. schedule a definite period of the work week for completing these forms and reports
    C. assign your foreman or cleaner to handle all these forms for you and to have them available on time
    D. classify or group the forms and reports and fill out only one of each group and refer the other forms or reports to the ones completed

16. A custodian engineer can BEST evaluate the quality of work performed by custodial personnel by

    A. periodic inspection of the building's cleanliness
    B. studying the time records of personnel
    C. reviewing the building cleaning expenditures
    D. analyzing complaints of building occupants

17. Assume that you are the custodian engineer and one of your employees wants to talk with you about a grievance. Of the following actions, the LEAST desirable action for you to take is to

    A. listen sympathetically
    B. conduct the discussion openly in the presence of the workforce
    C. try to get his point of view
    D. endeavor to obtain all the facts

18. Of the following factors, the one which is LEAST important in evaluating an employee and his work is his

    A. dependability   B. quantity of work done
    C. quality of work done   D. education and training

19. Supervision of a group of people engaged in building cleaning operations should NOT include supervision of

    A. time spent in cleaning operations
    B. utilization of official rest and lunch periods
    C. cleaning methods
    D. materials used for various cleaning jobs

20. Of the following methods, the BEST one to utilize in assigning custodial personnel to clean a multi-floor school building is to

    A. allow the cleaners to pick their room or area assignments out of a hat
    B. have the supervisor make specific room or area assignments to each cleaner separately
    C. rotate room and area assignments daily according to a chart posted on the bulletin board
    D. let a different member of the group make the room or area assignments each week

21. Assume that you are the custodian engineer and that you have discovered a bottle of liquor in one of your employee's locker.
The BEST course of action to take is to

   A. fire him immediately
   B. explain to him that liquor should not be brought into a school building and that a repetition may result
   C. in disciplinary action
   D. suspend him until the end of the week and take him back only on a probational basis
   E. assemble the staff and tell them they are all equally guilty for not having reported the matter to you

21.____

22. Of the following items, the one which is the LEAST important in the preparation of a report is that the report

   A. is brief, but to the point
   B. uses the prescribed form if there is one
   C. contains extra copies
   D. is accurate

22.____

23. In order to have building employees willing to follow standardized cleaning and maintenance procedures, the supervisor must be prepared to

   A. work alongside the employees
   B. demonstrate the reasonableness of the procedures
   C. offer incentive pay for their utilization
   D. allow the employees the free use of the time saved by their adoption

23.____

24. Suppose that you are the custodian engineer and one of your employees has gross earnings of $437.10 for the week, all of which is subject to deductions at the rate of 4.8%. The amount which should be deducted from the employee's gross earnings for the week is MOST NEARLY

   A. $2.10   B. $14.70   C. $17.70   D. $20.97

24.____

25. Suppose that you are a custodian engineer and an employee works for you at the rate of $8.70 per hour with time and one-half paid for time worked after 40 hours in one week. His gross pay for working 53 hours in one week is MOST NEARLY

   A. $461.10   B. $482.10   C. $487.65   D. $517.65

25.____

KEY (CORRECT ANSWERS)

1.	A	11.	A
2.	A	12.	C
3.	C	13.	C
4.	B	14.	D
5.	B	15.	B
6.	A	16.	A
7.	B	17.	B
8.	A	18.	D
9.	A	19.	B
10.	D	20.	B

21. B
22. C
23. B
24. D
25. D

TEST 4

DIRECTIONS: Each question or incomplete statement is followed by several suggested answers or completions. Select the one that BEST answers the question or completes the statement. *PRINT THE LETTER OF THE CORRECT ANSWER IN THE SPACE AT THE RIGHT.*

1. The minimum number of gate valves usually required in a by-pass around a steam trap is 1.____

    A. 1   B. 2   C. 3   D. 4

2. A 2-inch standard steel pipe, as compared with a 2-inch extra heavy steel pipe, has the same 2.____

    A. wall thickness
    B. inside diameter
    C. outside diameter
    D. weight per linear foot

3. A short piece of pipe with a standard male pipe thread on one end and a locknut thread on the other end is usually called a 3.____

    A. close nipple
    B. tank nipple
    C. coupling
    D. union

4. Dies are used by plumbers to 4.____

    A. ream out the inside of pipes
    B. thread pipes
    C. bevel the ends of pipes
    D. make up solder joints

5. Of the following types of pipe, the one which is MOST brittle is 5.____

    A. brass
    B. copper
    C. cast iron
    D. wrought iron

6. The PRIMARY function of a trap in a drainage system is 6.____

    A. prevent gases from flowing into the building
    B. produce an efficient flushing action
    C. prevent articles accidentally dropped into the drainage system from entering the water
    D. prevent the water backing up

7. If a plumbing fixture is allowed to stand unused for a long time, its trap is opt to lose its seal by 7.____

    A. evaporation
    B. capillary action
    C. siphonage
    D. condensation

8. The pipe fitting used to connect a 1 1/4" pipe directly to a 1" pipe in a straight line is called a 8.____

    A. union   B. nipple   C. elbow   D. reducer

9. The BEST procedure to follow when replacing a blown fuse is to

    A. immediately replace it with the same size fuse
    B. immediately replace it with a larger size fuse
    C. immediately replace it with a smaller size fuse
    D. correct the cause of the fuse failure and replace it with the correct size

10. The amperage rating of the fuse to be used in an electrical circuit is determined by the

    A. size of the connected load
    B. size of the wire in the circuit
    C. voltage of the circuit
    D. ambient temperature

11. In a 208-volt, 3-phase, 4-wire circuit, the voltage, in volts, from any line to the grounded neutral is approximately

    A. 208   B. 150   C. 120   D. zero

12. The device commonly used to change an A.C. voltage to a D.C. voltage is called a

    A. transformer   B. rectifier
    C. relay   D. capacitor or condenser

13. Where conduit enters a knock-out in an outlet box, it should be provided with a

    A. bushing on the inside and locknut on the outside
    B. locknut on the inside and bushing on the outside
    C. union on the outside and a nipple on the inside
    D. nipple on the outside and a union on the inside

14. The electric circuit to a ten kilowatt electric hot water heater which is automatically controlled by an aquastat will also require a

    A. transistor   B. choke coil
    C. magnetic contactor   D. limit switch

15. An electric power consumption meter usually indicates the power used in

    A. watts   B. volt-hours
    C. amperes   D. kilowatt-hours

16. Of the following sizes of copper wire, the one which can SAFELY carry the GREATEST amount of amperes is

    A. 14 ga. stranded   B. 12 ga. stranded
    C. 12 ga. solid   D. 10 ga. solid

17. A flexible coupling is PRIMARILY used to

    A. allow for imperfect alignment of two joining shafts
    B. allow for slight differences in shaft diameters
    C. insure perfect alignment of the joining shafts
    D. reduce fast starting of the machinery

18. The one of the following statements concerning lubricating oil which is CORRECT is:

    A. SAE 10 is heavier and more viscous than SAE 30
    B. diluting lubricating oil with gasoline increases its viscosity
    C. oil reduces friction between moving parts
    D. in hot weather, thin oil is preferable to heavy oil

19. The MAIN purpose of periodic inspections and tests made on mechanical equipment is to

    A. make the operating men familiar with the equipment
    B. keep the maintenance men busy during otherwise slack periods
    C. discover minor faults before they develop into serious breakdowns
    D. encourage the men to take better care of the equipment

20. The one of the following bearing types which is NOT classified as a roller bearing is

    A. radial   B. angular   C. thrust   D. babbit

21. In a wire rope, when a number of wires are laid left-handed into a strand and the strand laid right-handed around a hemp rope center, the wire rope is commonly known as a _____ rope.

    A. right-lay, Lang-lay   B. left-lay, Lang-lay
    C. left-lay, regular-lay   D. right-lay, regular-lay

22. The chemical which is NOT used for disinfecting swimming pools is

    A. ammonia   B. calcium hypochlorite
    C. chlorine   D. liquified chlorine

23. The one of the following V-belt sections which has the HIGHEST horsepower-per-belt rating is _____ section.

    A. A   B. B   C. C   D. D

24. An air compressor which is driven by an electric motor is usually started and stopped automatically by a(n)

    A. unloader   B. pressure regulator valve
    C. float switch   D. pressure switch

25. The volume, in cubic feet, of a cylindrical tank, 6 ft. in diameter x 35 ft. long is MOST NEARLY

    A. 210   B. 990   C. 1,260   D. 3,960

KEY (CORRECT ANSWERS)

1.	C	11.	C
2.	C	12.	B
3.	B	13.	A
4.	B	14.	C
5.	C	15.	D
6.	A	16.	D
7.	A	17.	A
8.	D	18.	C
9.	D	19.	C
10.	B	20.	D

21. D
22. A
23. D
24. D
25. B

EXAMINATION SECTION
TEST 1

DIRECTIONS: Each question or incomplete statement is followed by several suggested answers or completions. Select the one that BEST answers the question or completes the statement. *PRINT THE LETTER OF THE CORRECT ANSWER IN THE SPACE AT THE RIGHT.*

1. Of the following, the size of hard coal which is the SMALLEST is 1.____
   A. egg B. stove C. broken D. buckwheat

2. If the CO_2 content of the flue gases of an oil burner is very high, it USUALLY indicates 2.____
   A. too much oil admitted to the furnace
   B. good combustion of fuel
   C. good circulation of steam
   D. excessive steam production

3. When a steam radiator in a one-pipe gravity system is air-bound, the cause is MOST likely to be 3.____
   A. defective air valve
   B. air entering through a leaking line
   C. insufficient steam pressure
   D. defective gate valve

4. Of the following, the one which is MOST unlikely to cause warping or burning of grate bars is 4.____
   A. leaving gates uneven after shaking
   B. allowing free passage of air through the bars
   C. accumulating ashes in the ashpit
   D. shaking all ashes through to the ashpit in an active furnace

5. A wet return is BEST defined as a 5.____
   A. return line below the level of water in the boiler
   B. return that contains water as well as steam
   C. return that has an improper pitch causing backing up of water
   D. gravity return from which air has been removed

6. The MAIN supply of air for the burning of fuel in a coal-fired boiler enters through the _____ damper. 6.____
   A. fire door B. ashpit door C. breeching D. check

7. Steam traps are devices which serve to 7.____
   A. by-pass steam flow where radiators are filled with steam
   B. shut down rate of steam flow when steam temperature is too high
   C. separate air and condensate from steam in steam heating systems
   D. prevent the development of high steam pressures by releasing excess steam

8. When the diaphragm or bellows of a thermostatic radiator trap is found to be dirty, it is USUALLY cleaned with
   A. kerosene
   B. carbon tetrachloride
   C. mild soap and water
   D. turpentine

8.____

9. It is found that water is being carried over from an operating boiler into the steam main.
   Of the following, the one that is LEAST likely as the possible cause is
   A. water level higher than specified for the boiler
   B. grease and dirt in the boiler
   C. excessive rate of output
   D. insufficient installed radiation

9.____

10. Of the following, the PROPER step to take when firing a boiler by the coking method is to
    A. push the live coals to the rear of the grates and add fresh coal to the front part of the grates
    B. spread out the live coals and cover them frequently with a thin layer of fresh coal
    C. push the live coals to one side and place fresh coals on the other side, changing sides each time coal is added
    D. shovel the fresh coal on the rear of the grates and then cover them partly with live coals

10.____

11. Turpentine is added to paint MAINLY to
    A. enable it to dry more rapidly
    B. dissolve the pigment in the paint
    C. add corrosion resisting properties to the paint
    D. thin out the paint

11.____

12. Automatic operation of a sump pump is controlled by the
    A. electric switch
    B. float
    C. foot valve
    D. centrifugal driving unit

12.____

13. Kerosene costs 36 cents a quart.
    At that rate, two gallons would cost
    A. $1.44 B. $2.16 C. $2.88 D. $3.60

13.____

14. A PROPER procedure in the event of fire in a school building is to
    A. shut down all utilities—gas, electricity, and water
    B. maintain normal steam pressure in high pressure boilers equipped with auxiliaries driven by utility company electric power
    C. shut down all ventilating fans on central duct systems
    D. open all fire doors on the various floors to ventilate the fire

14.____

15. Piping used to carry electric wiring is COMMONLY called
    A. conduit B. leader C. conductor D. sleeve

15.____

16. The MAIN objection to using a copper penny in place of a blown fuse is that
    A. the penny will conduct electric current
    B. the penny will reduce the current flowing in the line
    C. melting of the penny will probably occur
    D. the line will not be protected against excessive current

16._____

17. A rip saw is GENERALLY used to cut
    A. corners
    B. uneven ragged lumber strips
    C. with the grain
    D. across the grain

17._____

18. Sweating USUALLY occurs in pipes that
    A. contain hot water
    B. contain cold water
    C. are chrome-plated
    D. require insulation

18._____

19. Workmen's Compensation insurance USUALLY provides
    A. employee benefits whether or not the injury was his fault
    B. employee benefits only if the employee was not negligent or exceptionally careless
    C. medical benefits in all cases, and compensation if no negligence or deliberate injury is found
    D. all benefits if absent from work four days or more

19._____

20. Of the following, the MOST important reason for making supply inventories is to
    A. schedule work assignments properly
    B. make certain that the supply room is in an orderly condition
    C. determine if employees are working efficiently
    D. check on the use of materials

20._____

21. Suppose that you are preparing a semi-annual requisition for janitorial supplies. The PROPER procedure in preparing the requisition is to
    A. order one and one-half times the amount actually needed to be sure of an adequate reserve
    B. order the amount actually needed as based on past use and probable needs
    C. ask each member of your staff to submit a statement of the supplies he will need
    D. order 10% more than the previous year to cover all possible emergencies

21._____

22. Beginning of period

22._____

End of period

The amount of gas, in cubic feet used during the measured period is
A. 183 B. 283 C. 362 D. 454

23. The MOST probable cause of foaming of a boiler that has been recently installed is
    A. poor draft
    B. higher than normal water level
    C. grease and oil in boiler
    D. excessive rate of output

23.____

24. When banking a fire, a PROPER step to take is to
    A. avoid any bright spots in the fuel bed
    B. close damper tightly
    C. open ashpit doors fully
    D. close fire doors

24.____

25. Of the following, the one which is considered POOR practice in boiler operation is keeping
    A. valves at the top and bottom of the water gauge glass open whenever operating boiler
    B. steam gauge cock open at all times when boiler is in operation
    C. fuel bed as light and shallow as possible to maintain fuel economy
    D. a thin ash layer over the grate to protect the bars from heat

25.____

26. A PROPER procedure in boiler operation is to blow down
    A. boilers and condensate tanks weekly
    B. the water column daily
    C. the water column weekly
    D. boilers only when necessary

26.____

27. The MAIN purpose of a condensate pump is to
    A. return water from the return lines to a boiler
    B. pump make-up water to maintain water level
    C. maintain steam pressure in the supply lines
    D. provide for continuous draining of radiators under pressure

27.____

28. In an oil-fired plant, the emergency or remote control switch is USUALLY located
    A. at the entrance to the boiler room
    B. next to the oil burner
    C. at the panel board in the boiler room
    D. at the electrical distribution panel for the building

28.____

29. A safety switch which is COMMONLY used in oil burner operation to detect flame failure and shut down the burner is a
    A. thermostat   B. stackswitch   C. aquastat   D. yulatrol

30. Of the following items, the one that has LEAST relation to the ignition system of an automatic horizontal rotary cup oil burner is a
    A. transformer   B. electrode
    C. gas valve   D. oil metering valve

31. The pressure of oil in the oil supply piping to a rotary cup oil burner is about 40 pounds.
    This pressure is maintained MAINLY in order to
    A. bring the oil into the atomizing cup
    B. mix the oil together with the primary air
    C. operate the magnetic oil valve
    D. avoid having the oil spray strike the edge of the oil nozzle

32. The atomizing cup of an oil burner shows carbon deposits.
    Of the following, the MOST desirable way to remove these deposits is to
    A. use a scraper, followed by light rubbing with 00 sandpaper
    B. wash the cup and nozzle with a mild trisodium phosphate solution and dry with a cloth
    C. use kerosene to loosen the deposits and wipe with a soft cloth
    D. apply a hot flame to the carbonized surfaces to burn off the carbon deposits

33. The MAJOR purpose of keeping the boiler filled with water during the non-heating season is that
    A. corrosion of interior parts will be prevented
    B. leaks in the boiler or piping will be detected more easily before the heating season begins
    C. no time will be lost in filling the boiler when the heating season starts
    D. scale deposits and impurities in the water will be reduced to a minimum

34. A MAJOR disadvantage of self-closing faucets in lines operating under moderate water pressure is that they
    A. close too rapidly
    B. frequently produce water hammer
    C. open too easily
    D. tend to become filled with sediment

35. When lamps are wired in parallel, the failure of one lamp will
    A. break the electric circuit to the other lamps
    B. have no effect on the power supply to the other lamps
    C. increase noticeably the light production of the other lamps
    D. cause excessive current to flow through the other lamps

36. A cotter pin is used to
    A. set tile
    B. reduce bushings
    C. strengthen bolts to stand a greater pull
    D. keep a nut from working loose

37. Of the following valves, the one which is automatic in operation is
    A. check   B. globe   C. angle   D. gate

38. The name of a fitting used to make a turn in the direction of a pipe line is
    A. union   B. bushing   C. elbow   D. coupling

39. If the flush tank of a water-closet fixture overflows, the fault is likely to be
    A. failure of the ball to seat properly
    B. excessive water pressure
    C. defective trap in the toilet bowl
    D. water-logged float

40. For the purpose of fire prevention, it is MOST important that the custodian
    A. know how to attack fires whatever their size
    B. detect and eliminate every possible fire hazard
    C. train his staff to place inflammables in fireproof containers
    D. see that halls, corridors, and exits are not blocked

41. In addition to his utilitarian duties and responsibilities, the custodian shall have general responsibility to assist the educational system by developing the cultural function of environment. This should follow automatically if his utilitarian work is well accomplished.
    This statement means MOST NEARLY that
    A. the custodian must act as a teacher of school children as well as operating and maintaining his building in accordance with highest standards
    B. if a custodian observes a teacher neglecting to discipline children properly, it is his duty to correct this failure
    C. the custodian must train his staff just as the educational system teaches children so that both achieve a higher cultural level
    D. if a custodian operates and maintains his building properly, he will assist in enabling teachers to do a better job

42. When you hire a new employee and you are preparing to train him in the work he is to perform, the FIRST thing to do is to
    A. tell him what his job is and find out what he already knows about it
    B. prepare a written description of the tasks the employee is to do and have him study them
    C. make certain that the employee has all the proper tools and materials and knows how to store them
    D. have him work along with another older employee to learn the requirements of the job

43. A cleaner tells you that several teachers do not keep their rooms clean, resulting in extra work for him.
Assuming that he is correct in his claim, the MOST desirable step to take is to
    A. visit the teachers directly and ask them to manage their classes so as to avoid excessive cleaning
    B. suggest to the principal that he discuss this cleaning problem with his teaching staff
    C. advise the cleaner to discuss the matter with the teachers involved
    D. tell the cleaner that nothing can be done and that he will just have to do the extra cleaning

43._____

44. When a repair is required in your school, the FIRST thing to do is to
    A. determine if you and your staff can handle it
    B. ask for assistance from the repair shop
    C. find out exactly what has to be done
    D. make a list of the materials and tools needed

44._____

45. A teacher complains to you that one of your staff failed to acknowledge his greeting and was not a very pleasant person.
The MOST reasonable thing to do is to
    A. tell the teacher that the employee does his work well and that is all you can ask of him
    B. advise the teacher to speak to the school principal if he has any real grievance
    C. tell the employee to be more polite to the teacher or he may lose his job
    D. discuss with your staff the need for a more friendly attitude toward the teaching staff

45._____

46. A cleaner asks to have his hours of work changed. You find that you cannot grant this request because you require coverage during those hours.
Under the circumstances, you should
    A. tell the cleaner that you cannot grant his request because the main office frowns on schedule changes
    B. deny his request and give your reasons for such denial
    C. advise the cleaner that if you changed his hours, other employees might make similar requests
    D. tell the cleaner that he should try to find another job with hours suitable to his needs

46._____

47. The purpose of a safety valve on a steam boiler is to
    A. start the feed pump when the water is low
    B. dampen the fire when the boiler is overheated
    C. shut off the feed pump when enough water is let into the boiler
    D. release the steam when the pressure gets too great

47._____

48. A device which is LEAST likely to be found in low pressure heating plants is a(n)
    A. vacuum pump
    B. inverted bucket trap
    C. economizer
    D. Hartford return connection

48._____

49. Baffle plates are sometimes put into furnaces to 49.____
    A. change the direction of heated gases
    B. increase the combustion of the fuel
    C. retard the burning of the gases
    D. prevent overloading of the combustion chamber

50. An operating boiler explosion may be caused by 50.____
    A. accumulation of gas in the furnace
    B. too deep a fire
    C. overpressure of steam
    D. too much water in the boiler

KEY (CORRECT ANSWERS)

1.	D	11.	D	21.	B	31.	A	41.	D
2.	B	12.	B	22.	C	32.	C	42.	A
3.	A	13.	C	23.	C	33.	A	43.	B
4.	B	14.	C	24.	D	34.	B	44.	C
5.	A	15.	A	25.	C	35.	B	45.	D
6.	B	16.	D	26.	B	36.	D	46.	B
7.	C	17.	C	27.	A	37.	A	47.	D
8.	A	18.	B	28.	A	38.	C	48.	C
9.	D	19.	A	29.	B	39.	D	49.	A
10.	A	20.	D	30.	D	40.	B	50.	C

TEST 2

DIRECTIONS: Each question consists of a statement. You are to indicate whether the statement is TRUE (T) or FALSE (F). *PRINT THE LETTER OF THE CORRECT ANSWER IN THE SPACE AT THE RIGHT.*

1. The amount of furniture in a classroom determines to a large extent the time that will be required to sweep it.   1.____

2. Exterior bronze should be wiped periodically with a soft cloth dampened with a light oil such as lemon oil.   2.____

3. A gallon of kerosene is heavier than a gallon of water.   3.____

4. The purpose of boiler feedwater treatment compound added to boiler water is to eliminate minor leaks in the boiler shell.   4.____

5. Air pockets occur more frequently in one-pipe heating systems than in two-piece systems.   5.____

6. Floor brushes should always be hung on pegs when not in use.   6.____

7. A floor brush, when used on a classroom floor, will stir up more dust than a good corn broom.   7.____

8. When sweeping a classroom with fixed desks and seats, the cleaner should use push strokes rather than pull strokes whenever possible.   8.____

9. Stick shellac is often used to fill in scratches and dents in furniture.   9.____

10. Although an ammonia solution is a good glass cleanser, it may darken the putty or painted frames of windows.   10.____

11. Chamois skins should be completely dry if they are to be used to dry windows or exterior glass.   11.____

12. The portable vacuum cleaner used in a school can be applied effectively to remove soot from boiler tubes.   12.____

13. If classroom floors are cleaned by means of a heavy-duty vacuum cleaner, they need not be cleaned daily.   13.____

14. Calcimined ceilings should be washed with lukewarm water occasionally to remove the accumulated dirt.   14.____

15. Corn brooms should be we with warm water once or twice a week to keep the fibers flexible.   15.____

16. A good time to wash windows is when the sun is shining on them.   16.____

17. When a floor is to be mopped, the cleaner should plan to mop only small areas at a time.   17.____

18. When mopping, the mop stroke used should be wide enough so that the mop can touch the baseboards of the room.   18.____

19. Toilet room odors tend to become more noticeable as the temperature of the room goes down.   19.____

20. Sweeping of a toilet floor should usually start at the door entrance and end at the far corner of the room.   20.____

21. When a mopping job is finished, the floor should be practically dry.   21.____

22. Dirt should be cleaned out from behind radiators before a classroom or corridor is swept.   22.____

23. When grease is to be dissolved in a clogged drain, it is more desirable to use lye than caustic polish.   23.____

24. A purpose for which school classrooms are oiled is to help preserve the wood.   24.____

25. It usually takes less time to sweep an oiled wood floor than an unoiled wood floor.   25.____

26. It is a good idea to soak new mop heads in boiling water for a short time before using them.   26.____

27. A desirable way to remove dry paint from glass is to use a very fine sandpaper.   27.____

28. A nail comb is commonly used to clean grease and dirt from the surfaces of nails.   28.____

29. A force cup or *plumbers friend* is used to remove obstructions in plumbing fixtures.   29.____

30. Panic bolts are usually found attached to swing-type window frames.   30.____

31. Good conductors of heat make good insulating material for covering hot water piping.   31.____

32. Slate blackboards in classrooms should usually be washed once a week.   32.____

33. A soda-acid fire extinguisher must be recharged after each use, no matter how slightly it has been used.   33.____

34. It is not practical to varnish wood floors in schools because the varnish coat is soon marred by heavy traffic.   34._____

35. A circular motion in washing and drying window glass is a more rapid and efficient method than a back-and-forth method.   35._____

36. The highest number visible on a steam gauge indicates the maximum allowable pressure in the boiler.   36._____

37. The outside doors of school buildings should open inward.   37._____

38. For interior building wiring, No. 14 wire is usually thicker than No. 12 wire.   38._____

39. Natural ventilation is obtained by adjusting the openings of windows and transoms.   39._____

40. Floor hair brushes should, in general, be kept dry because water tends to ruin them.   40._____

41. Wood floors should be mopped across the grain whenever possible.   41._____

42. Pails filled with cleaning solutions for mopping a floor should be placed on a wet space to prevent rings.   42._____

43. To effectively clean linoleum floors, very hot water should be used.   43._____

44. Cork tile requires a sealer coat before it is waxed for the first time.   44._____

45. The time it should take to dust the furniture of an average classroom each morning is about 5 or 6 minutes.   45._____

46. High dusting of classrooms should follow dusting of chairs, desks, and window sills.   46._____

47. Flathead screws should be countersunk into the material fastened.   47._____

48. The size of a nut is given by the diameter and number of threads per inch of the bolt it fits.   48._____

49. A good practice in boiler operation is to remove ashes from ashpits once a week during the heating season.   49._____

50. A transformer is a device used to raise or lower A.C. voltage.   50._____

KEY (CORRECT ANSWERS)

1.	T	11.	F	21.	T	31.	F	41.	F
2.	T	12.	T	22.	T	32.	T	42.	T
3.	F	13.	F	23.	F	33.	T	43.	F
4.	F	14.	F	24.	T	34.	T	44.	T
5.	F	15.	T	25.	T	35.	F	45.	T
6.	T	16.	F	26.	T	36.	F	46.	F
7.	F	17.	T	27.	F	37.	F	47.	T
8.	T	18.	F	28.	F	38.	F	48.	T
9.	T	19.	F	29.	T	39.	T	49.	F
10.	T	20.	F	30.	F	40.	T	50.	T

TEST 3

DIRECTIONS: Each question consists of a statement. You are to indicate whether the statement is TRUE (T) or FALSE (F). *PRINT THE LETTER OF THE CORRECT ANSWER IN THE SPACE AT THE RIGHT.*

1. White spots on waxed woodwork due to water or dampness may be removed with alcohol. 1.____

2. A counter brush should not be used to sweep under radiators or lockers. 2.____

3. A good way to dispose of waste paper in a school building is to burn the paper in the steam heating furnace. 3.____

4. Oxalic acid can be used to remove ink stains and rust from woodwork. 4.____

5. A desirable method of removing fingerprints and hardened dirt from porcelain fixtures is to apply a strong coarse powder cleanser. 5.____

6. Wet mop filler replacements are ordered by the weight of the filler, not the length of the strands. 6.____

7. A desirable method of controlling unpleasant odors in a washroom is to use pungent deodorants. 7.____

8. Fuses for branch lighting circuits are usually rated in watts. 8.____

9. The main purpose of oil in a bearing is to prevent the metal parts from touching. 9.____

10. Metal lighting fixtures should not be washed, but should be dusted and wiped lightly with a damp cloth. 10.____

11. The washing of painted walls should begin at the top and proceed down to the bottom of the wall. 11.____

12. Check valves are used to control the direction of flow of water or steam. 12.____

13. A blow-off valve on a boiler is used mainly to reduce steam pressure. 13.____

14. A wood floor should be slightly damp from washing immediately before oil is sprayed on it. 14.____

15. If an oil sprayer nozzle is rusty and gummy, it should be soaked in kerosene for a few days. 15.____

16. Chest x-ray examinations are required for school employees to check on their heart condition. 16.____

17. Auditoriums and assembly rooms usually require brighter lighting than gymnasiums. 17._____

18. The national flag should be displayed on every school day, but not on legal holidays. 18._____

19. The soda-acid fire extinguisher is not affected by freezing temperatures. 19._____

20. Clear cold water should be used to rinse rubber tile floors after they have been mopped. 20._____

21. New asphalt tile floors require the use of a sealer or lacquer to seal the pores. 21._____

22. Soapsuds are often used to locate gas leaks in gas lines. 22._____

23. A kilowatt equals 1000 watts. 23._____

24. The very first step a custodian should take when a water pipe bursts is to call for a plumber. 24._____

25. *Rock Island Sheepswool* is a term usually applied to natural sponges. 25._____

26. There is less danger of electric shock when electric wires are touched with wet hands than with dry hands. 26._____

27. Air for ventilation of school buildings should never be recirculated. 27._____

28. Sweeping compound for use on linoleum and asphalt tile should contain sawdust, floor oil, and water wax. 28._____

29. Chlordane is useful as an insecticide for the control of crawling insects such as roaches. 29._____

30. Soda-acid fire extinguishers for use in school buildings usually have a gallon capacity. 30._____

31. Kick plates of doors should be lubricated about once a month. 31._____

32. A stillson wrench is usually used on heads and nuts of bolts. 32._____

33. No. 000 steel wool is coarser than No. 0 steel wool. 33._____

34. The preferred type of paint for the walls of school classrooms is a durable glossy enamel. 34._____

35. More accidents result from unsafe actions than from unsafe conditions. 35._____

3 (#3)

36. The steam gauge cock should always be open when the boiler is operating.   36._____

37. When a wire carrying current becomes hot, it indicates that the fuse in the line has blown.   37._____

38. If the fusible plug of a boiler is coated with scale, it will melt at a lower temperature.   38._____

39. A water pump is usually primed with oil or grease.   39._____

40. Sharp-edged hand tools should usually be carried with the sharp edge down.   40._____

41. Using chisels with mushroomed heads is a safe practice if the user wears safety goggles.   41._____

42. The fire in a boiler furnace should be cleaned before banking it for the night.   42._____

43. School classrooms usually require weekly scrubbing in order to keep them acceptably clean.   43._____

44. Trisodium phosphate is a poor cleaning agent for oily or greasy surfaces.   44._____

45. Weathering of coal is a source of fuel waste.   45._____

46. Standpipes usually supply water to the toilets and fountains on the upper floors of a building.   46._____

47. Goods subject to damage by heat should be stored near the ceiling of a storeroom if possible.   47._____

48. Two light coats of wax on a floor are better than one good heavy coat.   48._____

49. If a custodian sees a child defacing a corridor wall, he should not stop the child but should report him to the principal or teacher.   49._____

50. A carbon tetrachloride fire extinguisher can be effectively used to put out a fire in an electric motor.   50._____

KEY (CORRECT ANSWERS)

1.	T	11.	F	21.	F	31.	F	41.	F
2.	F	12.	T	22.	T	32.	F	42.	T
3.	F	13.	F	23.	T	33.	F	43.	F
4.	T	14.	F	24.	F	34.	F	44.	F
5.	F	15.	T	25.	T	35.	T	45.	T
6.	T	16.	F	26.	F	36.	T	46.	F
7.	F	17.	F	27.	F	37.	F	47.	F
8.	F	18.	F	28.	F	38.	F	48.	T
9.	T	19.	F	29.	T	39.	F	49.	F
10.	T	20.	T	30.	T	40.	T	50.	T

EXAMINATION SECTION

TEST 1

DIRECTIONS: Each question or incomplete statement is followed by several suggested answers or completions. Select the one that BEST answers the question or completes the statement. *PRINT THE LETTER OF THE CORRECT ANSWER IN THE SPACE AT THE RIGHT.*

1. In the wintertime, the FIRST thing a custodian does in the morning, after throwing the main switch, is to
   A. take a reading of the electric meter
   B. prepare his daily report of fuel consumption
   C. prepare sweeping compound
   D. inspect the water gauge of his boilers

   1.____

2. Rubbish, stones, sticks, and papers on lawns in front of school buildings are MOST effectively collected by means of a
   A. 30 inch floor brush with thickly set bristles
   B. corn broom
   C. 4 foot pole with a nail set in the bottom of it
   D. rake

   2.____

3. Which of the following statements about sweeping is NOT correct?
   A. Corridors and stairs should not be swept during school hours.
   B. Classrooms should usually be swept daily after the close of the afternoon session.
   C. Dry sweeping is not to be used in classrooms or corridors.
   D. Special rooms, as sewing rooms, may be swept during school hours if unoccupied.

   3.____

4. The PROPER size of floor brush to be used in classrooms with fixed seats is _____ inches.
   A. 36   B. 24   C. 16   D. 6

   4.____

5. Sweeping compound made of oiled sawdust should NOT be used on _____ floors.
   A. cement   B. rubber tile
   C. oiled wood   D. composition

   5.____

6. In oiling a wood floor, it is GOOD practice to
   A. apply the oil with a dipped mop up to the baseboards of the walls
   B. avoid application of oil closer than 6 inches of the baseboards
   C. keep the oil about one inch from the baseboard
   D. make sure that oil is applied to the floors under radiators

   6.____

7. Of the following, the LEAST desirable agent for cleaning blackboards is 7.____
   A. damp cloth
   B. clear warm water applied with a sponge
   C. warm water with a little kerosene
   D. warm water containing a mild soap solution

8. Chalk trays of blackboards should be washed and cleaned 8.____
   A. once a week
   B. daily
   C. only when the teacher reports cleaning needed
   D. once a month

9. In cleaning rooms by means of a central vacuum cleaning system, 9.____
   A. sweeping compound is used merely to prevent dust from rising
   B. rooms need cleaning only twice a week because the machine takes up the oil
   C. wood floors must be oiled more frequently as the machine takes up the oil
   D. the cleaner should not press down upon the tool but should guide it across the floor

10. A gas leak is suspected in the home economics class of a school. 10.____
    The procedure in locating the leak is to
    A. use a lighted match
    B. use a safety lamp
    C. place nose close to line and smell each section
    D. use soapsuds

11. The MOST important reason for placing asbestos jackets on steam lines is to 11.____
    A. prevent persons from burning their hands
    B. prevent heat loss
    C. protect the lines from injury
    D. make the lines appear more presentable

12. If the flag is used on a speaker's platform, it should be displayed 12.____
    A. above and behind the speaker
    B. as a drape over the front of the platform
    C. as a rosette over the speaker's head
    D. as a cover over the speaker's desk

13. When the flag of the United States of America is displayed from a staff 13.____
    projecting from the front of the building, it should be
    A. extended to the tip of the staff
    B. extended to about one foot from the tip of the staff
    C. secured so that there is a sag in the line
    D. extended slowly to the tip of the staff and then drawn back rapidly about 15 inches

14. The common soda-acid fire extinguisher should be checked and refilled 14.____
    A. every week   B. every month
    C. once a year   D. only if used

15. A small fire has broken out in an electric motor in a sump pump. The 15.____
    lubricant has apparently caught fire.
    The PROPER extinguisher to use is
    A. sand
    B. carbon tetrachloride (pyrene) fire extinguisher
    C. soda-acid fire extinguisher
    D. water under pressure from a hose

16. While cleaning windows, an employee falls from the fourth floor of the building 16.____
    to the sidewalk. The custodian finds the man unconscious.
    The custodian should
    A. move the man into a more comfortable position near the wall of the
       building and then call a doctor
    B. try to revive the man by depressing his head slightly and applying artificial
       respiration
    C. hail a taxi and bring the man to a hospital for treatment
    D. phone for an ambulance and cover the man to keep him warm

17. The duties of a custodian include the knowledge of safety rules to prevent 17.____
    accidents and injuries to his employees and himself.
    Of the following, the LEAST harmful practice is to
    A. carry a scraper in the pocket with the blade down
    B. measure the cleaning powder with your hands before placing the powder
       in water
    C. wet the hands before using steel wool
    D. use lye to clean paint brushes

18. The MOST important reason for not wringing out a mop by hand is that 18.____
    A. water cannot be removed effectively in this way
    B. it is not fair to the cleaner
    C. the dirt remains on the mop after the water is removed
    D. pins, nail, or other sharp objects may be picked up and cut the hand,
       causing an infection

19. The method of using a ladder which you would consider LEAST safe is: 19.____
    A. Grasping the side rails of the ladder instead of the rungs when going up
    B. To see that the door is secured wide open when working on a ladder at a
       door
    C. Leaning weight toward ladder while working on it
    D. Standing on top of the ladder to reach working place

20. When a window pane is broken, the FIRST step the custodian takes is to 20.____
    A. remove broken glass from floors and window sill
    B. determine the cause

C. remove the putty with a putty knife
D. prepare a piece of glass to replace the broken pane

21. Your instructions to a cleaner about the proper sweeping of offices should include the following instruction: 21.____
    A. Do not move chairs and wastebaskets from their places when sweeping
    B. Place chairs and baskets on the desks to get them out of the way
    C. Set aside the loose small furniture and chairs in an orderly manner when sweeping office floors
    D. Move the desks and chair to the side of the room close to the wall in order to sweep properly

22. To remove dirt accumulations after the completion of the sweeping task, brushes should be 22.____
    A. tapped on the floor in the normal sweeping position
    B. struck on the floor against the side of the block
    C. struck on the floor against the end of the block
    D. turned upside down and the handle tapped on the floor

23. To sweep rough cement floors in a basement, the BEST tool to use is a 23.____
    A. deck brush   B. new 30" floor brush
    C. corn broom   D. treated mop

24. When a floor is scrubbed, it is NOT correct to 24.____
    A. use a steady, even rotary motion
    B. rinse the floor with clean hot water
    C. have the mop strokes follow the boards when drying the floor
    D. wet the floor first by pouring several bucketsful of water on it

25. Flushing with a hose is MOST appropriate as a method of cleaning 25.____
    A. terrazzo floors of corridors
    B. untreated wood floors
    C. linoleum floor where not in frequent use
    D. cement floors

KEY (CORRECT ANSWERS)

1.	D	11.	B
2.	D	12.	A
3.	A	13.	A
4.	C	14.	C
5.	B	15.	B
6.	D	16.	D
7.	C	17.	A
8.	A	18.	D
9.	D	19.	D
10.	D	20.	A

21. C
22. A
23. C
24. D
25. D

TEST 2

DIRECTIONS: Each question or incomplete statement is followed by several suggested answers or completions. Select the one that BEST answers the question or completes the statement. *PRINT THE LETTER OF THE CORRECT ANSWER IN THE SPACE AT THE RIGHT.*

Questions 1-5.

DIRECTIONS: Column I lists cleaning jobs. Column II lists cleansing agents and devices. Select the proper cleansing agent from Column II for each job in Column I. Place the letter of the cleansing agent selected in the space at the right corresponding to the number of the cleansing job.

	COLUMN I		COLUMN II	
1.	Chewing gum	A.	Muriatic acid	1.____
2.	Ink stains	B.	Broad bladed knife	2.____
3.	Fingermarks on glass	C.	Kerosene	3.____
4.	Rust stains on porcelain	D.	Oxalic acid	4.____
5.	Hardened dirt on porcelain	E.	Lye	5.____
		F.	Linseed oil	

6. When the bristles of a floor brush have worn short, the brush should be   6.____
   A. thrown away and the handles saved
   B. saved and the brush used on rough cement floors
   C. saved and used for high dusting in classrooms
   D. saved and used for the weekly scrubbing of linoleum floors

7. Feather dusters should NOT be used because they   7.____
   A. take more time to use than other dusters
   B. cannot be cleaned
   C. do not take up the dust but merely move it from one place to another
   D. do not stir up the dust and streak the furniture with dust rails

8. Floors that are usually NOT waxed are those made of   8.____
   A. pine wood   B. mastic tile   C. rubber tile   D. terrazzo

9. For sweeping under radiators and other inaccessible places, the MOST appropriate tool is the   9.____
   A. counter brush   B. dry mop
   C. feather duster   D. 16" floor brush

10. A cleansing agent that should NOT be used in the cleaning of windows is
    A. water containing fine pumice
    B. water containing a small amount of ammonia
    C. water containing a little kerosene
    D. a paste cleanser made from water and cleaning powder

11. The BEST way to dust desks is to use a
    A. circular motion with soft dry cloth that has been washed
    B. damp cloth, taking care not to disturb papers on the desk
    C. soft cloth, moistened with oil, using a back and forth motion
    D. back and forth motion with a soft dry cloth

12. Trisodium phosphate is a substance BEST used in
    A. washing kalsomined walls
    B. polishing of brass
    C. washing mastic tile floors
    D. clearing stoppages

13. Treated linoleum is PROPERLY cleaned by daily
    A. dusting with a treated mop
    B. sweeping with a floor brush
    C. mopping with a weak soap solution
    D. mopping after removal of dust with a floor brush

14. Of the following, the MOST proper use for chamois skin is
    A. drying of window glass after washing
    B. washing of window glass
    C. polishing of metal fixtures
    D. drying toilet bowls after washing

15. A squeegee is a tool which is used in
    A. clearing stoppage in waste lines
    B. the central vacuum cleaning system
    C. cleaning inside boiler surfaces
    D. drying windows after washing

16. Concrete and cement floors are usually painted a battleship gray color. The MOST important reason for painting the floor is
    A. to improve the appearance of the floor
    B. the paint prevents the absorption of too much water when the floor is mopped
    C. the paint makes the floor safer and less slippery
    D. the concrete becomes harder and will not settle

17. After a sweeping assignment is completed, floor brushes should be stored
    A. in the normal sweeping position, bristles resting on the floor
    B. by hanging the brushes on pegs or nails
    C. by piling the brushes on each other carefully in a horizontal position
    D. in a dry place after a daily washing

18. Painted walls and ceilings should be brushed down
    A. daily
    B. weekly
    C. every month, especially during the winter
    D. two or three times a year

19. If an asphalt tile floor becomes excessively dirty, the method of cleaning should include
    A. the use of kerosene or benzene as a solvent
    B. the use of a solution of modified laundry soda
    C. sanding down the spotted areas with a sanding machine on the wet floor
    D. use of a light oil and treated mop

20. To remove light stains from marble walls, the BEST method is to
    A. use steel wool and a scouring powder, then rinse with clear warm water
    B. wash the stained area with a dilute acid solution
    C. sand down the spot first, then wash with mild soap solution
    D. wet marble first, then scrub with mild soap solution using a soft fiber brush

21. To rid a toilet room of objectionable odors, the PROPER method is to
    A. spread some chloride of lime on the floor
    B. place deodorizer cubes in a box hung on the wall
    C. wash the floor with hot water containing a little kerosene
    D. wash the floor with hot water into which some disinfectant has been poured

22. Toilet rooms, to be cleaned properly, should be swept
    A. daily
    B. and mopped daily
    C. daily and mopped twice a week
    D. daily and mopped thoroughly at the end of the week

23. In waxing a floor, it is usually BEST to
    A. start the waxing under stationary furniture and then do the aisles
    B. pour the wax on the floor, spreading it under the desks with a wax mop
    C. remove the old wax coat before rewaxing
    D. wet mop the floor after the second coat has dried to obtain a high polish

24. The BEST reason why water should not be used to clean kalsomined walls of a boiler room is that the
    A. walls are usually not smooth and will hold too much water
    B. kalsomine coating does not hold dust
    C. kalsomine coating will dissolve in water and leave streaks
    D. wall brick and kalsomine coating will not dissolve in water and so cannot be cleaned

25. In mopping a floor, it is BEST practice to   25.____
    A. swing the mop from side to side, using the widest possible stroke across the floor up to the baseboard
    B. swing the mop from side to side, using the widest possible stroke across the floor surface, stopping the stroke from 3 to 5 inches from baseboards
    C. use short, straight strokes, up and back, stopping the strokes about 5 inches from the baseboard
    D. use short straight strokes, up and back, stopping the strokes at the baseboards

KEY (CORRECT ANSWERS)

1.	B	11.	D
2.	D	12.	C
3.	C	13.	A
4.	A	14.	A
5.	C	15.	D
6.	B	16.	B
7.	C	17.	B
8.	D	18.	D
9.	A	19.	D
10	A	20.	D

21.	D
22.	B
23.	A
24.	C
25.	B

EXAMINATION SECTION
TEST 1

DIRECTIONS: Each question or incomplete statement is followed by several suggested answers or completions. Select the one that BEST answers the question or completes the statement. *PRINT THE LETTER OF THE CORRECT ANSWER IN THE SPACE AT THE RIGHT.*

1. Of the following, the BEST way for you to make sure that a cleaner understands a spoken order which you have given to him is for you to
   A. ask him to repeat the order in his own words
   B. ask him whether he has understood the order
   C. watch how he begins to follow the order
   D. ask him whether he has any questions about the order

   1.____

2. You have called a meeting with your cleaners to get their suggestions on ways to keep up cleaning standards in spite of budget cutbacks.
   You will MOST likely be successful in encouraging them to participate in the discussion if you
   A. start the meeting by giving the cleaners all your own suggestions first
   B. keep the meeting going by talking whenever the cleaners have nothing to say
   C. get the cleaners to *think out loud* by asking them for their interpretations of the problem
   D. comment on and evaluate the suggestions made by each cleaner immediately after he makes them

   2.____

3. If a custodian knows that rumor being spread by his assistants are false, he should
   A. tell the assistants that the rumors are false
   B. tell the assistants the facts which the rumors have falsified
   C. threaten to discipline any assistant who spreads the rumors
   D. find out which assistant started the rumor and have him suspended

   3.____

4. One of your cleaners tells you in private that he wants to quit his job.
   The FIRST thing you should do in handling this matter is to
   A. ask the cleaner why he wants to quit his job
   B. tell the cleaner to take a few days to think it over
   C. refer the cleaner to the personnel office
   D. try to convince the cleaner not to quit his job

   4.____

5. The MOST important reason why a custodian should seek the suggestions of his cleaners on job-related matters is that the
   A. cleaners generally have greater knowledge of job-related matters than the custodian
   B. cleaners will tend to have a greater feeling of participation in their jobs by making suggestions

   5.____

C. custodians will be able to hold the cleaners responsible for any suggestions he follows
D. custodians can win the respect of his cleaners by showing them the errors in their suggestions

6. Your supervisor has ordered you to announce to your cleaners a new cleaning rule with which you disagree.
You should
   A. admit honestly to your cleaners that you disagree with the rule
   B. announce the rule to your cleaners without expressing your disagreement
   C. encourage your cleaners by telling them you agree with the rule
   D. tell your supervisor that you refuse to announce any rule with which you disagree

7. Of the following, the BEST practice to follow in criticizing the work performance of a cleaner is to
   A. save up several criticisms and make them all at one time
   B. soften your criticism by being humorous
   C. have another cleaner, who has more seniority, give the criticism
   D. make sure that you explain to the cleaner the reasons for your criticism

8. Of the following, the BEST way to reduce unnecessary absences among your cleaners is to
   A. ask your cleaners the reason for their absence every time they are absent
   B. rely entirely on written warnings once every month to cleaners who have been absent too often during the month
   C. have your cleaners make a formal written report to you every time they are absent, explaining the reason for their absence
   D. threaten to fire your cleaners every time they are absent

9. A group of students complains to you about the lack of cleanliness in your building. You realize that budget cutbacks are unavoidably led to shortages in manpower and equipment for the cleaning staff.
Of the following, the BEST way for you to answer these students is to
   A. tell them frankly that the cleanliness of the building is none of their business as students
   B. apologize for the condition of the building and promise that your men will work harder
   C. tell them to take their complaints to the administration and not to you
   D. explain the reasons for the building's condition and what you are doing to improve it

10. The MOST important role of the school custodian in promoting public relations in the community should be to help
    A. increase understanding between the custodial staff and the community which it serves
    B. keep from community attention any failings on the part of the custodial staff

C. increase the authority of the custodial staff over the community with which it deals
D. keep the community from interfering in the operations of the custodial staff

11. A teacher conducting a class calls you to complain that the cleaners cleaning the empty classroom next to hers are being unnecessarily noisy.
Of the following, the BEST response to the teacher is to tell her that
   A. she should go next door to tell the cleaners to stop the unnecessary noise
   B. you will tell the cleaners about her complaint and instruct them not to make unnecessary noise
   C. she should file a formal complaint against the cleaners with your superior
   D. you will come to her classroom to judge for yourself whether the cleaners are being unnecessarily noisy

11.____

12. The attitude a school custodian should generally maintain toward the faculty and students is one of
   A. avoidance   B. superiority   C. courtesy   D. servility

12.____

13. The flow of oil in an automatic rotary cup oil burner is regulated by a(n)
   A. thermostat   B. metering valve
   C. pressure relief valve   D. electric eye

13.____

14. The one of the following devices that is required on both coal-fired and oil-fired boilers is a(n)
   A. safety valve   B. low water cut-off
   C. feedwater regulator   D. electrostatic precipitator

14.____

15. The type of fuel which must be preheated before it can be burned efficiently is
   A. natural gas   B. pea coal
   C. number 2 oil   D. number 6 oil

15.____

16. A suction gauge in a fuel-oil transfer system is USUALLY located
   A. before the strainer
   B. after the strainer and before the pump
   C. after the pump and before the pressure relief valve
   D. after the pressure relief valve

16.____

17. The FIRST item that should be checked before starting the fire in a steam boiler is the
   A. thermostat   B. vacuum pump
   C. boiler water level   D. feedwater regulator

17.____

18. Operation of a boiler that has been *sealed* by the Department of Buildings is
   A. prohibited
   B. permitted when the outside temperature if below 32ºF
   C. permitted between the hours of 6:00 A.M. and 8:00 A.M. and 9:00 P.M. and 11:00 P.M.
   D. permitted only for the purpose of heating domestic water

18.____

19. Lowering the thermostat setting by 5 degrees during the heating season will result in fuel savings of MOST NEARLY _____ percent.
    A. 2 B. 5 C. 20 D. 50

20. An electrically-driven rotary fuel oil pump MUST be protected from internal damage by the installation in the oil line of a
    A. discharge side strainer
    B. check valve
    C. suction gauge
    D. pressure relief valve

21. A float-thermostatic steam trap in a condensate return line that is operating properly will allow
    A. steam and air to pass and will hold back condensate
    B. air and condensate to pass and will hold back steam
    C. steam and condensate to pass and will hold back air
    D. steam to pass and will hold back air and condensate

22. Changes in the combustion efficiency of a boiler can be determined by comparing changes in stack temperature and
    A. steam pressure in the header
    B. over the fire draft
    C. percentage of carbon dioxide
    D. equivalent of direct radiation

23. The classification of the coal that is USUALLY burned in a city school building is
    A. anthracite
    B. bituminous
    C. semi-bituminous
    D. lignite

24. A boiler is equipped with the following pressuretrols:
    I. Manual-reset   II. Modulating   III. High-limit
    The CORRECT sequence in which these devices should be actuated by rising steam pressure is
    A. I, II, III B. II, III, I C. III, I, II D. III, II, I

25. The temperature of the returning condensate in a low-pressure steam heating system if 195°F.
    This temperature indicates that
    A. some radiator traps are defective
    B. some boiler tubes are leaking
    C. the boiler water level is too low
    D. there is a high vacuum in the return line

26. An over-the-fire draft gauge in a natural draft furnace is USUALLY read in
    A. feet per minute
    B. pounds per square inch
    C. inches of mercury
    D. inches of water

27. The Air Pollution Code states that no person shall cause or permit the emission of an air contaminant of a density which appears as dark or darker than number ____ on the standard smoke chart.
    A. one B. two C. three D. four

28. The equipment which is used to provide tempered fresh air to certain areas of a school building is a(n)
    A. exhaust fan
    B. window fan
    C. fixed louvre
    D. heating stack

    28.____

29. When a glass globe is put back over a newly replaced lightbulb in a ceiling light fixture, the holding screws on the globe should be tightened, then loosened, one half turn.
    This is done MAINLY to prevent
    A. fires caused by electrical short circuits
    B. cracking of the globe due to heat expansion
    C. falling of the globe from the light fixture
    D. building up of harmful gases inside the globe

    29.____

30. Standard 120 volt type fuses are GENERALLY rated in
    A. farads   B. ohms   C. watts   D. amperes

    30.____

31. A cleaner informs you that his electric vacuum cleaner is not working even though he tried the off-on switch several times and checked to see that the plug was still in the wall outlet.
    Of the following, the FIRST course of action you should take in this situation is to
    A. determine if the circuit breaker has tripped out
    B. take apart the vacuum cleaner
    C. replace the electric cord on the vacuum cleaner
    D. replace the electrical outlet

    31.____

32. The one of the following that is the MOST practical method for a school custodian to use in making a temporary repair in a straight portion of a water pipe which has a small leak is to
    A. attach a clamped patch over the leak
    B. weld or braze the pipe, depending on the material
    C. drill and tap the pipe, then insert a plug
    D. fill the hole with an epoxy sealer

    32.____

33. The PRIMARY function of the packing which is generally found in the stuffing box of a centrifugal pump is to
    A. compensate for misalignment of the pump shaft
    B. prevent leakage of the fluid
    C. control the discharge rate of the pump
    D. provide support for the pump shaft

    33.____

34. Of the following, the MOST important reason for replacing a worn washer in a dripping faucet as soon as possible is to prevent
    A. overflow of the sink trap
    B. the mixture of hot and cold water in the sink
    C. damage to the faucet parts that can be the result of overtightening the stem
    D. air from entering the supply line

    34.____

35. In carpentry work, the MOST commonly used hand saw is the _____ saw.   35.____
    A. hack   B. rip   C. buck   D. cross-cut

36. The device which USUALLY keeps a doorknob from rotating on the spindle is a   36.____
    A. cotter pin   B. tapered key
    C. set screw   D. stop screw

37. The following tasks are frequently done when an office is cleaned: 37.____
    I. The floor is vacuumed.
    II. The ashtrays and wastebaskets are emptied.
    III. The desks and furniture are dusted.
    The order in which these tasks should GENERALL be done is
    A. I, II, III   B. II, III, I   C. III, II, I   D. I, III, II

38. When wax is applied to a floor by the use of a twine mop with a handle, the   38.____
    wax should be _____ with the mop.
    A. applied in thin coats
    B. applied in heavy coats
    C. poured on the floor, then spread
    D. dripped on the floor, then spread

39. The BEST way to clean dust from an acoustical type ceiling is with a   39.____
    A. strong soap solution   B. wet sponge
    C. vacuum cleaner   D. stream of water

40. Of the following, the MOST important reason why a wet mop should NOT be   40.____
    wrung out by hand is that
    A. the strings of the mop will be damaged by hand-wringing
    B. sharp objects picked up by the mop may injure the hands
    C. the mop cannot be made dry enough by hand-wringing
    D. fine dirt will become embedded in the strings of the mop

KEY (CORRECT ANSWERS)

1.	A	11.	B	21.	B	31.	A
2.	C	12.	C	22.	C	32.	A
3.	B	13.	B	23.	A	33.	B
4.	A	14.	A	24.	B	34.	C
5.	B	15.	D	25.	A	35.	D
6.	B	16.	B	26.	D	36.	C
7.	D	17.	C	27.	D	37.	B
8.	A	18.	A	28.	B	38.	A
9.	D	19.	C	29.	B	39.	C
10.	A	20.	B	30.	D	40.	B

TEST 2

DIRECTIONS: Each question or incomplete statement is followed by several suggested answers or completions. Select the one that BEST answers the question or completes the statement. *PRINT THE LETTER OF THE CORRECT ANSWER IN THE SPACE AT THE RIGHT.*

1. When a painted wall is washed by hand, the wall should be washed from the _____ with a _____ sponge. 1.____
   A. top down; soaking wet
   B. bottom up; soaking wet
   C. top down; damp
   D. bottom up; damp

2. When a painted wall is brushed with a clean lambswool duster, the duster should be drawn _____ with _____ pressure. 2.____
   A. downward; light
   B. upward; light
   C. downward; firm
   D. upward; firm

3. The one of the following items which BEST describes the size of a floor brush is 3.____
   A. 72 cubic inch
   B. 32 ounce
   C. 24 inch
   D. 10 square foot

4. When a slate blackboard is washed by hand, it is BEST to use 4.____
   A. a mild soap solution and allow the blackboard to air dry
   B. warm water and allow the blackboard to air dry
   C. a mild soap solution and sponge the blackboard dry
   D. warm water and sponge the blackboard dry

5. The MAIN reason why the handle of a reversible floor brush should be shifted from one side of the brush lock to the opposite side is to 5.____
   A. change the angle at which the brush sweeps the floor
   B. give equal wear to both sides of the brush
   C. permit the brush to sweep hard-to-reach areas
   D. make it easier to sweep blackboard

6. When a long corridor is swept with a floor brush, it is good practice to 6.____
   A. push the brush with moderately long strokes and flick it after each stroke
   B. press on the brush and push it the whole length of the corridor in one sweep
   C. pull the brush inward with short, brisk strokes
   D. sweep across rather than down the length of the corrido

7. Of the following office cleaning jobs performed during the year, the one which should be done MOST frequently is 7.____
   A. cleaning the fluorescent lights
   B. dusting the Venetian blinds
   C. cleaning the bookcase glass
   D. carpet-sweeping the rug

8. The BEST polishing agent to use on wood furniture is 8.____
   A. pumice B. paste wax
   C. water emulsion wax D. neatfoot's oil

9. Lemon oil polish is used BEST to polish 9.____
   A. exterior bronze B. marble walls
   C. lacquered metal floors D. leather seats

10. Cleaning with trisodium phosphate will MOST likely damage 10.____
    A. toilet bowls B. drain pipes
    C. polished marble floors D. rubber tile floors

11. Of the following cleaning agents, the one which should NOT be used is 11.____
    A. caustic lye B. detergent
    C. scouring powder D. ammonia

12. The one of the following cleaners which GENERALLY contains an abrasive is 12.____
    A. caustic lye B. trisodium phosphate
    C. scouring powder D. ammonia

13. The instructions on a box of cleaning powder say, *Mix one pound of cleaning powder in four gallons of water.* 13.____
    According to these instructions, how many ounces of cleaning powder should be mixed in one gallon of water?
    A. 4 B. 8 C. 12 D. 16

14. In accordance with recommended practice, a dust mop, when not used, should be stored 14.____
    A. hanging, handle end down
    B. hanging, handle end up
    C. standing on the floor, handle end down
    D. standing on the floor, handle end up

15. The two types of floors found in public buildings are classified as *hard* and *soft* floors. 15.____
    An example of a hard floor is one made of
    A. linoleum B. cork C. ceramic tile D. asphalt tile

16. The BEST way for a custodian to determine whether a cleaner is doing his work well is by 16.____
    A. observing the cleaner a work for several hours
    B. asking the cleaner questions about the work
    C. asking other cleaners to rate his work
    D. inspecting the cleanliness of the spaces assigned to the cleaner

17. A chemical frequently used to melt ice on outdoor pavements is 17.____
    A. ammonia B. soda
    C. carbon tetrachloride D. calcium chloride

18. A herbicide is a chemical PRIMARILY used as a(n) 18.____
    A. disinfectant   B. fertilizer
    C. insect killer   D. weed killer

19. Established plants that continue to blossom year after year without reseeding 19.____
    are GENERALLY known as
    A. annuals   B. parasites   C. perennials   D. symbiotics

20. A ferrous sulfate solution is sometimes used to treat shrubs or trees that 20.____
    have a deficiency of
    A. boton   B. copper   C. iron   D. zinc

21. A tree described is deciduous. 21.____
    This means PRIMARILY that it
    A. bears nuts instead of fruit   B. has been pruned recently
    C. usually grows in swampy ground   D. loses its leaves in fall

22. If you are told that a container holds a 20-7-7 fertilizer, it is MOST likely that 22.____
    twenty percent of this fertilizer is
    A. nitrogen   B. oxygen
    C. phosphoric acid   D. potash

23. When the national flag is in such a worn condition that it is no longer a fitting 23.____
    emblem for display, it should be disposed of by
    A. bagging inconspicuously with other disposables
    B. burning in an inconspicuous place
    C. laundering and then using it for cleaning purposes
    D. storing for future use as a painters dropcloth

24. The landscape drawings for a school indicate the planting of *Acer platanoides* 24.____
    at a certain location on the grounds.
    Acer platanoides is a type of
    A. privet hedge   B. rose bush
    C. maple tree   D. tulip bed

25. Improper use of a carbon dioxide type portable fire extinguisher may cause 25.____
    injury to the operator because
    A. handling the nozzle during discharge can cause frostbite to the skin
    B. carbon dioxide is highly poisonous if breathed into the lungs
    C. use of carbon dioxide on a oil fire can cause a chemical explosion
    D. of the extremely high pressures inside the extinguisher

26. When using a portable single ladder with ten rungs, the GREATEST number 26.____
    of rungs that a cleaner should climb up is
    A. 7   B. 8   C. 9   D. 10

27. Of the following types of portable fire extinguishers, the one which should be used to control a fire in or around live electrical equipment is the _____ type.
    A. foam
    B. soda acid
    C. carbon dioxide
    D. gas cartridge water

27._____

28. The MOST frequent cause of accidental injuries to workers on the job is
    A. unsafe working practices of employees
    B. poor design of buildings and working areas
    C. lack of warning signs in hazardous working areas
    D. lack of adequate safety guards on equipment and machinery

28._____

29. Of the following, the MOST important purpose of preparing an accident report on an injury to a cleaner is to help
    A. collect statistics on different types of accidents
    B. calm the feelings of the injured cleaner
    C. prevent similar accidents in the future
    D. prove that the cleaner was at fault

29._____

30. A cleaner is attempting to lift a heavy drum of liquid cleaner from the floor to a shelf at waist height.
    He will MOST likely avoid personal injury in lifting the drum if he
    A. keeps his back as straight as possible and lift the weight
    B. arches his back and lifts the weight primarily with his back muscles
    C. keeps his back as straight as possible and lifts the weight primarily with his leg muscles
    D. arches his back and lifts the weight primarily with his leg muscles

30._____

31. Of the following, the BEST first aid treatment for a cleaner who has burned his hand with dry caustic lye crystals is to
    A. wash his hand with large quantities of warm water
    B. brush his hand lightly with a soft, clean brush and wrap it in a clean rag
    C. place his hand in a mild solution of ammonia and cool water
    D. wash his hand with large quantities of cold water

31._____

32. The purpose of the third prong in a three-prong electric plug used on a 120-volt electric vacuum cleaner is to prevent
    A. serious overheating of the vacuum cleaner
    B. electric shock to the operator of the vacuum cleaner
    C. generation of dangerous microwaves by the vacuum cleaner
    D. sparking in the electric outlet caused by a loose electrical wire

32._____

33. Of the following, the LEAST effective method for a school custodian to use to reduce window glass breakage in his school is to
    A. keep the area near the school free of sticks and stones
    B. consult with parents and civic organizations and request their assistance in reducing breakage

33._____

C. request that neighbors living near the school report afterhours incidents to the police department
D. develop a reputation as a *tough guy* with the students so that they will be afraid to break windows in the school

34. The one of the following procedures that a school custodian should use when a telephone caller makes a threat to place a bomb in the school is to
    A. hang up on the caller
    B. keep the caller talking as long as possible and make notes on what he says
    C. tell the caller he has the wrong number
    D. tell the caller his voice is being recorded and the call is being traced to its source

35. A school custodian is responsible for enforcing certain safety regulations in the school.
    The MOST important reason for enforcing safety regulations is because
    A. every accident can be prevented
    B. compliance with safety regulations will make all other safety efforts unnecessary
    C. safety regulations are the law and law enforcement is an end in itself
    D. safety regulations are based on reason and experience with the best methods of accident prevention

36. The safety belts that are worn by cleaners when washing outside windows should be inspected
    A. before each use   B. weekly
    C. monthly   D. semi-annually

37. The one of the following actions that a school custodian should take to help reduce burglary losses in the school is to
    A. leave all the lights on in the school overnight
    B. see that interior and exterior doors are securely locked
    C. set booby traps that will severely injure anyone breaking in
    D. set up an apartment in the school basement and stay at the school every night

38. The one of the following types of locks that is used on emergency exit doors is a _____ bolt.
    A. panic   B. dead   C. cinch   D. toggle

39. A telephone caller tells a school custodian that a bomb has been placed in the building and immediately hangs up the phone.
    The FIRST thing the school custodian should do, in the absence of the principal, is to
    A. call the fire department
    B. call the police department
    C. let his subordinate handle it
    D. ignore the call, since most threats are hoaxes

40. If an employee's bi-weekly salary is $1,200.00 and 6.7% is withheld for taxes, the amount to be withheld for this purpose is MOST NEARLY 40.____
   A. $62.00   B. $66.00   C. $82.00   D. $74.00

KEY (CORRECT ANSWERS)

1.	D	11.	A	21.	D	31.	D
2.	A	12.	C	22.	A	32.	B
3.	C	13.	A	23.	B	33.	D
4.	B	14.	B	24.	C	34.	B
5.	B	15.	C	25.	A	35.	D
6.	A	16.	D	26.	B	36.	A
7.	D	17.	D	27.	C	37.	B
8.	B	18.	D	28.	A	38.	A
9.	A	19.	C	29.	C	39.	B
10.	C	20.	C	30.	C	40.	C

EXAMINATION SECTION
TEST 1

DIRECTIONS: Each question or incomplete statement is followed by several suggested answers or completions. Select the one that BEST answers the question or completes the statement. *PRINT THE LETTER OF THE CORRECT ANSWER IN THE SPACE AT THE RIGHT.*

1. A custodian was given a booklet that showed a new work method that could save time. He didn't tell his men because he thought that they would get the booklet anyway. For the custodian to have acted like this is a

    A. *good* idea, because he saves the time and bother of talking to the men
    B. *bad* idea, because he should make sure his men know about better work methods
    C. *good* idea, because the men would rather read about it themselves
    D. *bad* idea, because a supervisor should always show his men every memo he gets from higher authority

    1.____

2. A custodian found it necessary to discipline two subordinates. One man had been operating his equipment in a wrong way, while the other man came to work late for three days in a row. The supervisor decided to talk to both men together.
   For the custodian to deal with the problems in this way is a

    A. *good* idea, because each man will learn about the difficulties of the other person and how to solve such difficulties
    B. *bad* idea, because the supervisor should wait until he can bring a larger group together and save time in discussing such questions
    C. *good* idea, because he will be able to get the men to see that their problems are related
    D. *bad* idea, because he should meet with each man separately and give him his full attention

    2.____

3. A custodian should try to make his men feel their jobs are important in order to

    A. get the men to say good things about their supervisor to his own superior
    B. get the men to think in terms of advancing to better jobs
    C. let higher management in the agency know that the supervisor is efficient
    D. help the men to be able to work more efficiently and enthusiastically

    3.____

4. A custodian should know approximately how long it takes to do a particular kind of job CHIEFLY because he

    A. will know how much time to take if he has to do it himself
    B. will be able to tell his men to do it even faster
    C. can judge the performance of the person doing the job
    D. can retrain experienced employees in better work habits

    4.____

5. Custodians often get their employees' opinions about better work methods because

    A. the men will know that they are respected
    B. the men would otherwise lose all their confidence in the supervisor
    C. the supervisor might find in this way a good suggestion he could use
    D. this is the best method for improvement of work methods

    5.____

6. Right after you have trained your subordinates in doing a new job, you find that they seem to be doing all right, but that it will take them several days to finish. You also have several groups of men working at other locations. The MOST efficient way for you to make sure that the men continue doing the new job properly is to

   A. stay on that job with the men until it is finished, just in case trouble develops
   B. visit the men every half hour until the job is done
   C. stay away from their job that day, and visit the men the next day to ask them if they had any problems
   D. visit the men a few times each day until they finish the new job

7. Assume that one of your new employees is older than you are. You also think that he may be hard to get along with because he is older than you.
   The BEST way for you to avoid any problems with the older worker is for you to

   A. *lay down the law* immediately and tell the man he better not cause you any trouble
   B. treat the man just the way you would any other worker
   C. always ask the older worker for advice in the presence of all the men
   D. ignore the man entirely until he realizes that you are the boss

8. Assume you have tried a new method suggested by one of your employees, and find that it is easier and cheaper than the method you had been using.
   The proper thing for you to do NEXT is to

   A. say nothing to anyone, but train your men to use the new method
   B. train your men to use the new method and tell your crew that you got the idea from one of the men
   C. continue using the old method, because a supervisor should not use suggestions of his men
   D. have your crew learn the new method and take credit for the idea since you are the boss

9. Suppose you are a custodian and your superior tells you that the way your men are doing a certain procedure is wrong and that you should re-train your men as soon as possible. When you begin to re-train the men, the FIRST thing you should do is

   A. tell your men that a wrong procedure had been used and that a new method must be learned as a result
   B. train your employees in the new method with no explanation, since you are the boss
   C. tell the crew that your superior has just decided that everyone should learn a new method
   D. tell the crew that your superior says your method is wrong, but that you don't agree with this

10. It is *bad* practice to criticize a man in front of the other men because

    A. people will think you are too strict
    B. it is annoying to anyone who walks by
    C. it is embarrassing to the man concerned
    D. it will antagonize the other men

11. A custodian decides not to put his two best men on a work detail because he knows that they won't like it.
    For the custodian to make the work assignment this way is a

    A. *good* idea, because it is only fair to give your best men a break once in a while
    B. *bad* idea, because you should treat all of your men fairly and not show favoritism
    C. *good* idea, because you save the strength of these men for another job
    D. *bad* idea, because more of the men should be exempted from the assignment

11.____

12. Suppose you are a custodian and you find it inconvenient to obey an established procedure set by your agency. You think another procedure would be better.
    The BEST thing to do FIRST about this procedure that you don't like is for you to

    A. obey the procedure even if you don't want to, and suggest your idea to your own supervisor
    B. disregard the procedure because a supervisor is supposed to have some privileges
    C. follow the procedure some of the time, but ignore it when the men aren't watching
    D. organize a group of other supervisors to get the procedure changed

12.____

13. A custodian estimated that it would take his crew one workday per week to do a certain job each week. However, after a month he noticed that the job averaged two-and-a-half days a week, and this delayed other jobs that had to be done.
    The FIRST thing that the custodian should do in this case is to

    A. call his men together and warn them that they will get a poor work evaluation if they don't work harder
    B. talk to each man personally, asking him to work harder on the job
    C. go back and study the maintenance job by himself, to see if more men should be assigned to the job
    D. write his boss a report describing in detail how much time it is taking the men to do the job

13.____

14. An employee complains to you that some of his work assignments are too difficult to do alone.
    Which of the following is the BEST way for you to handle this complaint?

    A. Go with him to see exactly what he does and why he finds it so difficult.
    B. Politely tell the man that he has to do the job or be brought up on charges.
    C. Tell the man to send his complaint to the head of your agency.
    D. Sympathize with the man and give him easier jobs.

14.____

15. The BEST way for a custodian to keep control of his work assignments is to

    A. ask the men to report to him immediately when their jobs are finished
    B. walk around the buildings once a week, and get a first-hand view of what is being done
    C. keep his ears open for problems and complaints, but leave the men alone to do the work
    D. write up a work schedule, and check it periodically against the actual work done

15.____

16. A custodian made a work schedule for his men. At the bottom of it he wrote, *No changes or exceptions will be made in this schedule for any reason.*
For the custodian to have made this statement is

    A. *good,* because the men will respect the custodian for his attitude
    B. *bad,* because there are emergencies and special situations that occur
    C. *good,* because each man will know exactly what is expected of him
    D. *bad,* because the men should expect that no changes will ever be made in the work schedule without written permission

17. Which one of the following would NOT be a result of a well-planned work schedule?
The schedule

    A. makes efficient use of the time of the staff
    B. acts as a checklist for an important job that might be left out
    C. will give an idea of the work to a substitute supervisor
    D. shows at a glance who the best men are

18. A new piece of equipment you have ordered is delivered. You are familiar with it but the men under you, who will use it, do not know the equipment.
Of the following methods, which is the BEST to take in explaining to them how to operate this equipment?

    A. Ask the men to watch other crews using the equipment
    B. Show one reliable man how to operate the equipment and ask him to teach the other men
    C. Ask the men to read the instructions in the manual for the equipment
    D. Call the men together and show them how to operate the equipment

19. One custodian assigns work to his men by calling his crew together each week and describing what has to be done that week. He then tells them to arrange individual assignments among themselves and to work as a team during the week.
This method of scheduling work is a

    A. *good* idea, because this guarantees that the men will work together
    B. *bad* idea, because responsibility for doing the job is poorly fixed
    C. *good* idea, because the men will finish the job in less tirae working together
    D. *bad* idea, because the supervisor should always stay with his men

20. Suppose that a custodial assistant came to the custodian with a problem concerning his assignment.
For the custodian to listen to this problem is a

    A. *good* idea, because a supervisor should always take time off to talk when one of his men wants to talk
    B. *bad* idea, because the supervisor should not be bothered during the work day
    C. *good* idea, because it's the job of the supervisor to deal with problems of job assignment
    D. *bad* idea, because the employee could start annoying the supervisor with all sorts of problems

21. Suppose that on the previous afternoon you were looking for an experienced employee in order to give him an emergency job and he was missing from his job location. The next morning he tells you that he got sick suddenly and had to go home, but couldn't tell you since you weren't around. He has never done this before.
What should you do?

    A. Tell the man he is excused and that in such circumstances he did the wisest thing.
    B. Bring the man up on charges because, whatever he says, he could still have notified you.
    C. Have the man examined by a doctor to see if he really was sick the day before
    D. Explain to the man that he should make every effort to tell or to get a message to you if he must leave

22. An employee had a grievance and went to the custodian about it. The employee wasn't satisfied with the way the custodian tried to help him, and told him so. Yet the custodian had done everything he could under the circumstances.
The PROPER action for the supervisor to take at this time is to

    A. politely tell the employee that there is nothing more for the custodian to do about the problem
    B. let the employee know how he can bring his complaint to a higher authority
    C. tell the employee that he must solve the problem on his own, since he didn't want to follow the custodian's advice
    D. suggest to the employee that he ask another supervisor for assistance

23. In which of the following situations is it BEST to give your men spoken rather than written orders?

    A. You want your men to have a record of the instructions.
    B. Spoken instructions are less likely to be forgotten.
    C. An emergency situation has arisen in which there is no time to write up instructions.
    D. There are instructions on time and leave regulations which are complicated.

24. One of your employees tells you that a week ago he had a small accident on the job, but he didn't bother telling you because he was able to continue working.
For the employee not to have told the custodian about the accident was

    A. *good,* because the accident was a small one
    B. *bad,* because all accidents should be reported, no matter how small
    C. *good,* because the custodian should be bothered only for important matters
    D. *bad,* because having an accident is one way to get excused for the day

25. For a custodian to deal with each of his subordinates in exactly the same manner is

    A. *poor,* because each man presents a different problem and there is no other way of handling all problems
    B. *good,* because once a problem is handled with one man, he can handle another man with the same problem
    C. *poor,* because the men will resent it if they are not handled each in a better way than others
    D. *good,* because this assures fair and impartial treatment of each subordinate

KEY (CORRECT ANSWERS)

1. B
2. D
3. D
4. C
5. C

6. D
7. B
8. B
9. A
10. C

11. B
12. A
13. C
14. A
15. D

16. B
17. D
18. D
19. B
20. C

21. D
22. B
23. C
24. B
25. A

TEST 2

DIRECTIONS: Each question or incomplete statement is followed by several suggested answers or completions. Select the one that BEST answers the question or completes the statement. *PRINT THE LETTER OF THE CORRECT ANSWER IN THE SPACE AT THE RIGHT.*

1. One day a custodial assistant said to the custodian, *I can get a tile cleaner that is as good as the stuff we use, and for less money, because my brother is a building contractor. How about it?*
   The CORRECT way for the custodian to handle this situation is for him to

   A. thank the assistant, but tell him that individual workers cannot buy their own cleaning material for project use
   B. tell the assistant that no one has any right to start interfering in the buying procedures of the authority
   C. go along with the assistant and buy the cleaner from his brother, because it might save money for the authority
   D. tell the assistant to have his brother contact the project manager

2. A new custodial assistant under your supervision is waxing a floor for the first time. While the job seems to be going along well, he is not doing it quite the way you asked him to do it and so is taking longer than he should. Which of the following is the BEST action for you to take under these conditions?

   A. Leave him to finish the job and go on to the next one
   B. Interrupt him and tell him to do the job the way he was taught
   C. Tell him he is doing well but that he should do better
   D. Explain to him why your way is faster and tell him to try it

3. The easiest way for a custodian to find out how many supplies are available is to

   A. look at last year's figures
   B. keep an up-to-date inventory
   C. ask one of the men to let you know
   D. check the availability when he uses a special item

4. Of the following, the MOST likely result of a report that has been planned well is that it will

   A. explain, in detail, general procedures of supervision
   B. be read by most of the top officials of the department
   C. have some award-winning suggestions
   D. state the facts in a clear, orderly way

5. It is better to make a written report, instead of a face-to-face report, when

   A. you expect your superior to have questions about what is in the report right away
   B. your superior wants to know about your work immediately
   C. the report is very short
   D. you will have to give your report to many people in different locations

6. Of the following, the MOST important fact a custodian should include in an accident report is

   A. the name of the insurance company of the injured person
   B. cost to the city of the accident
   C. name and address of the injured person
   D. your idea for preventing such an accident in the future

7. Making an outline of the contents of a long report, before writing the report, is often a good idea. The advantage is that

   A. you can file an outline to refer to it in the future
   B. your supervisor can see it and know that you are working on the report
   C. you can make the outline a part of your report
   D. it will help you in writing the report

8. Of the following, the MOST important reason for the custodian's making detailed reports in all accidents is to

   A. have a record of who is at fault in case lawsuits should result
   B. be better able to estimate the cost of the accident
   C. reduce the number of compensation claims
   D. determine the cause of the accident and prevent future accidents

9. A custodian's written instructions to his staff on the subject of security in public buildings should include instructions to

   A. exclude the public at all times
   B. admit the public at all times
   C. admit the public only if they are neat and well-dressed
   D. admit the public during specified hours

10. The key figure in any custodial safety program is the

    A. building custodian   B. cleaner
    C. operating engineer   D. commissioner

11. A supervisor should know the equipment used in his work well enough to

    A. make any repairs which might be needed
    B. know what parts to remove in case of breakdown
    C. anticipate any reasonable possibility of a breakdown
    D. know all the lubricants specified by the manufacturer

12. The PRIMARY responsibility of a building custodian is to

    A. make friends of all subordinates
    B. search for new methods of doing the work
    C. win the respect of his superior
    D. get the work done properly within a reasonable time

13. If the directions given by your superior are not clear, the BEST thing for you to do is to

A. ask to have the directions repeated and clarified
B. proceed to do the work taking a chance on doing the right thing
C. do nothing until some later time when you can find out exactly what is wanted
D. ask one of the other men in your crew what he would do under the circumstances

14. Of the following procedures concerning grievances of subordinate personnel, the custodian-engineer should maintain an attitude on

    A. paying little attention to little grievances
    B. being very alert to grievances and make adjustments in existing conditions to appease all personnel
    C. knowing the most frequent causes of grievances and strive to prevent them from arising
    D. maintaining firm discipline of a nature that *smooths out* all grievances

15. Of the following, the BEST course of action to take to settle a dispute or conflict between two employees is to

    A. insist that the two employees settle the case between themselves
    B. call in each one separately and, after hearing their cases presented, decide the issue
    C. bring both in for a conference at the same time and make the decision in their presence
    D. have both present their points of view and arguments in written memoranda and on this basis make your decision

16. If, as a custodian-engineer, you discover an error in your report submitted to the main office, you should

    A. do nothing, since it is possible that one error will have little effect on the total report
    B. wait until the error is discovered in the main office and then offer to work overtime to correct it
    C. go directly to the supervisor in the main office after working hours and ask him unofficially to correct the error
    D. notify the main office immediately so that the error can be corrected, if necessary

17. There are a considerable number of forms and reports to be submitted on schedule by the custodian-engineer. The ADVISABLE method of accomplishing this duty is to

    A. fill out the reports at odd times during the days when you have free time
    B. schedule a definite period of the work week for completing these forms and reports
    C. assign your foreman or cleaner to handle all these forms for you and to have them available on time
    D. classify or group the forms and reports and fill out only one of each group and refer the other forms or reports to the ones completed

18. A custodian-engineer can BEST evaluate the quality of work performed by custodial personnel by

    A. periodic inspection of the building's cleanliness
    B. studying the time records of personnel
    C. reviewing the building cleaning expenditures
    D. analyzing complaints of building occupants

19. Assume that you are the custodian-engineer and one of your employees wants to talk with you about a grievance. Of the following actions, the LEAST desirable action for you to take is to

    A. listen sympathetically
    B. conduct the discussion openly in the presence of the workforce
    C. try to get his point of view
    D. endeavor to obtain all the facts

20. Of the following factors, the one which is LEAST important in evaluating an employee and his work is his

    A. dependability
    B. quantity of work
    C. quality of work
    D. education and training

21. Supervision of a group of people engaged in building cleaning operations should NOT include supervision of

    A. time spent in cleaning operations
    B. utilization of official rest and lunch periods
    C. cleaning methods
    D. materials used for various cleaning jobs

22. Of the following methods, the BEST one to utilize in assigning custodial personnel to clean a multi-floor school building is to

    A. allow the cleaners to pick their rooms or area assignments out of a hat
    B. have the supervisor make specific room or area assignments to each cleaner separately
    C. rotate room and area assignments daily according to a chart posted on the bulletin board
    D. let a different member of the group make the room or area assignments each week

23. Assume that you are the custodian-engineer and that you have discovered a bottle of liquor in one of your employees' locker. The BEST course of action to take is to

    A. fire him immediately
    B. explain to him that liquor should not be brought into a school building and that a repetition may result in disciplinary action
    C. suspend him until the end of the week and take him back only on a probational basis
    D. assemble the staff and tell them they are all equally guilty for not having reported the matter to you

24. Of the following items, the one which is the LEAST important in the preparation of a report is that the report

    A. is brief, but to the point
    B. uses the prescribed form if there is one
    C. contains extra copies
    D. is accurate

25. In order to have building employees willing to follow standardized cleaning and mainte- 25.____
nance procedures, the supervisor must be prepared to
   A. work alongside the employees
   B. demonstrate the reasonableness of the procedures
   C. offer incentive pay for their utilization
   D. allow the employees the free use of the time saved by their adoption

KEY (CORRECT ANSWERS)

1. A	11. C
2. D	12. D
3. B	13. A
4. B	14. C
5. D	15. C
6. C	16. D
7. D	17. B
8. D	18. A
9. D	19. B
10. A	20. D

21. B
22. B
23. B
24. C
25. B

READING COMPREHENSION
UNDERSTANDING AND INTERPRETING WRITTEN MATERIAL

EXAMINATION SECTION
TEST 1

DIRECTIONS: Each question or incomplete statement is followed by several suggested answers or completions. Select the one that BEST answers the question or completes the statement. *PRINT THE LETTER OF THE CORRECT ANSWER IN THE SPACE AT THE RIGHT.*

Questions 1-3.

DIRECTIONS: Questions 1 through 3 are to be answered in accordance with the following passage.

Terrazzo flooring will last a very long time if it is cared for properly. Lacquers, shellac, or varnish preparations should never be used on terrazzo. Soap cleaners are not recommended since they dull the appearance of the floor. Alkaline solutions are harmful, so a neutral cleaner or non-alkaline synthetic detergents will give best results. If the floor is very dirty, it may be necessary to scrub it. The same neutral cleaning solution should be used for scrubbing as for mopping. Scouring powder may be sprinkled at particularly dirty spots. Do not use steel wool for scrubbing. Small pieces of steel filings left on the floor will rust and dis-color the terrazzo. Non-woven nylon or open-mesh fabric abrasive pads are suitable for scrubbing terrazzo floors.

1. According to the passage above, the BEST cleaning agent for terrazzo flooring is a(n)

   A. soap cleaner B. varnish preparation
   C. neutral cleaner D. alkaline solution

2. According to the passage above, terrazzo floors should NOT be scrubbed with

   A. non-woven nylon abrasive pads
   B. steel wool
   C. open-mesh fabric abrasive pads
   D. scouring powder

3. As used in the passage above, the word *discolor* means MOST NEARLY

   A. crack B. scratch C. dissolve D. stain

Questions 4-7.

DIRECTIONS: Questions 4 through 7 are to be answered in accordance with the information given in the following passage.

MOPPING FLOORS

When mopping hardened cement floors, either painted or unpainted, a soap and water mixture should be used. This should be made by dissolving half a cup of soft soap in a pail of hot water. It is not desirable, however, under any circumstances, to use a soap and water mixture on cement floors that are not hardened. For mopping this type of floor, it is recommended that the cleaning agent be made up of 2 ounces of laundry soda mixed in a pail of water.

Soaps are not generally used on hard tile floors because slippery films may build up on the floor. It is generally recommended that these floors be mopped using a pail of hot water in which has been mixed 2 ounces of washing powder for each gallon of water. The floors should then be rinsed thoroughly.

After the mopping is finished, proper care should be taken of the mop. This is done by first cleaning the mop in clear warm water. Then, it should be wrung out, after which the strands of the mop should be untangled. Finally, the mop should be hung by its handle to dry.

4. According to the above passage, you should NEVER use a soap and water mixture when mopping _____ floors.

    A. hardened cement
    B. painted
    C. unhardened cement
    D. unpainted

4._____

5. According to the above passage, using laundry soda mixed in a pail of water as a cleaning agent is recommended for

    A. all floors
    B. all floors except hard tile floors
    C. some cement floors
    D. linoleum floor coverings *only*

5._____

6. According to the above passage, the GENERALLY recommended mixture for mopping hard tile floors is _____ of hot water.

    A. 1/2 cup of soft soap for each gallon
    B. 1/2 cup of soft soap in a pail
    C. 2 ounces of washing powder in a pail
    D. 2 ounces of washing powder for each gallon

6._____

7. According to the above passage, the PROPER care of a mop after it is used includes

    A. cleaning it in clear cold water and hanging it by its handle to dry
    B. wringing it out, untangling and drying it
    C. untangling its strands before wringing it out
    D. untangling its strands while cleaning it in clear water

7._____

Questions 8-15.

DIRECTIONS: Questions 8 through 15 are to be answered ONLY in accordance with the following paragraph.

Many custodial foremen have discovered through experience that there are economies to be *realized* by using discretion when ordering items which are similar to each other. For example, it may be cheaper to order a *Sponge block, cellulose, WET SIZE: 6 in. x 4 3/4 in. x APPROXIMATELY 34 inches long* at $7.00 than it is to order separate *Sponges, cellulose, wet size: 2 in. x 4 in. x 6 in.* at 60¢. It does not pay to *over-order* on floor wax which may turn sour if not used soon enough. An average size college building cannot afford to have extra 30-inch floor brooms costing $19.75 each stored *on the shelf* for a couple of years or to let moths destroy the hair in such brooms if proper safeguards are not used.

8. According to the above passage, the items mentioned which are *similar* are   8._____

   A. floor brooms
   B. sponges
   C. floor waxes
   D. moths

9. As used in the above paragraph, the term *over-order* means to   9._____

   A. order again
   B. back order
   C. order too little
   D. order too much

10. Of the items for which prices are given in the above paragraph, the MOST expensive one is the   10._____

    A. 30-inch floor broom
    B. 6 in. x 4 3/4 in. x 34 in. sponge block
    C. 2 in. x 4 in. x 6 in. sponge
    D. floor wax

11. As used in the above paragraph, the word *realized* means MOST NEARLY   11._____

    A. obtained   B. lost   C. equalized   D. cheapened

12. According to the above paragraph, the one of the following which may be damaged by moths is the   12._____

    A. floor broom
    B. sponge
    C. cellulose
    D. wool cloth

13. As used in the above paragraph, the term *wet size* means   13._____

    A. the chemical treatment given to sponges
    B. the amount of water the sponge can hold
    C. that the sponges must be kept moist at all times
    D. that the measurements given were taken when the sponges were wet

14. As used in the above paragraph, the word *at* means   14._____

    A. near   B. arrived   C. each   D. new

15. As used in the above paragraph, the word *approximately* means   15._____

    A. exactly   B. about   C. economical   D. tan

Questions 16-17.

DIRECTIONS: Questions 16 and 17 are to be answered in accordance with the following paragraph.

Painting is done to preserve surfaces; and unless the surface is properly prepared, good preservation will not be possible. Apply paint only to clean dry surfaces. After a surface has been scaled, which means that all loose paint and rust are removed by chipping, scraping, and wire brushing, be sure all dust and dirt are completely removed.

16. According to the above paragraph, the MAIN purpose of painting a wall is to _____ the wall.

    A. clean
    B. waterproof
    C. protect
    D. remove dust from

17. According to the above paragraph,

    A. chipping, scraping, and wire brushing are the only methods permitted for cleaning surfaces
    B. painting is effective only when the surface is clean
    C. scaling refers only to the removal of rust
    D. paint may be applied on wet surfaces

Questions 18-21.

DIRECTIONS: Questions 18 through 21 are to be answered SOLELY on the basis of the following paragraph.

All cleaning agents and supplies should be kept in a central storeroom which should be kept locked and only the custodian, store-keeper, and foreman should have keys. Shelving should be provided for the smaller items while barrels containing scouring powder or other bulk material should be set on the floor or on special cradles. Each compartment in the shelves should be marked plainly and only the item indicated stored therein. Each barrel should also be marked plainly. It may also be desirable to keep special items such as electric lamps, flashlight batteries, etc. in a locked cabinet or separate room to which only the custodian and the night building foreman have keys.

18. According to the above paragraph, scouring powder

    A. should be kept on shelves
    B. comes in one-pound cans
    C. should be kept in a locked cabinet
    D. is a bulk material

19. According to the above paragraph,

    A. the storekeeper should not be entrusted with the safekeeping of light bulbs
    B. flashlight batteries should be stored in barrels
    C. the central storeroom should be kept locked
    D. only special items should be stored under lock and key

20. According to the above paragraph,

    A. each shelf compartment should contain at least four different items
    B. barrels must be stored in cradles
    C. all items stored should be in marked compartments
    D. crates of light bulbs should be stored in cradles

21. As used in the above paragraph, the word *cradle* means a   21.____

    A. dolly
    B. support
    C. doll's bed
    D. hand truck

Questions 22-25.

DIRECTIONS: Questions 22 through 25 are to be answered SOLELY on the basis of the following paragraph.

There are on the market many cleaning agents for which amazing claims are made. Chemical analysis shows that the majority of them are well-known chemicals slightly modified and packaged and sold under various trade names. For that reason, the agents which have been selected for your use are those whose cleaning properties are well-known and whose use can be standardized. It is obviously undesirable to offer too wide a selection as that would be confusing to the cleaner, but a sufficient number must be provided so that a satisfactory agent is available for each task.

22. According to the above paragraph,   22.____

    A. there are few cleaning agents on the market
    B. there are no really good cleaning agents on the market
    C. cleaning agents are sold under several different brand names
    D. all cleaning agents are the same

23. According to the above paragraph,   23.____

    A. all cleaning agents should be chemically analyzed before use
    B. the best cleaning agents are those for which no claims are made by the manufacturer
    C. different cleaning agents may be needed for different tasks
    D. all cleaning agents have been standardized by the federal government

24. As used in the above paragraph, the word *amazing* means   24.____

    A. illegal
    B. untrue
    C. astonishing
    D. specific

25. As used in the above paragraph, the word *modified* means   25.____

    A. changed   B. refined   C. labelled   D. diluted

KEY (CORRECT ANSWERS)

1.	C	11.	A
2.	B	12.	A
3.	D	13.	D
4.	C	14.	C
5.	C	15.	B
6.	D	16.	C
7.	B	17.	B
8.	B	18.	D
9.	D	19.	C
10.	A	20.	C

21. B
22. C
23. C
24. C
25. A

TEST 2

Questions 1-3.

DIRECTIONS: Questions 1 through 3 are to be answered in accordance with the following passage. Each question or incomplete statement is followed by several suggested answers or completions. Select the one that BEST answers the question or completes the statement. *PRINT THE LETTER OF THE CORRECT ANSWER IN THE SPACE AT THE RIGHT.*

The method of cleaning which should generally be used is the space assignment method. Under this method, the buildings to be cleaned are divided into different sections. Within each section, each crew of Custodial Assistants is assigned to do one particular cleaning job. For example, within a section, one crew may be assigned to cleaning offices, another to scrubbing floors, a third to collecting trash, and so on. Other methods which may be used are the post assignment method and the gang cleaning method. Under the post assignment method, a Custodial Assistant is assigned to one area of a building and performs all cleaning jobs in that area. This method is seldom used except where buildings are so small and distant from each other that it is not economical to use the space assignment method. Under the gang cleaning method, a Custodial Foreman takes a number of Custodial Assistants through a section of the building. These Custodial Assistants work as a group and complete the various cleaning jobs as they go. This method is generally used only where the building contains very large open areas.

1. According to the passage above, under the space assignment method, each crew GENERALLY   1.____

    A. works as a group and does a variety of different cleaning jobs
    B. is assigned to one area and performs all cleaning jobs in that area
    C. does one particular cleaning job within a section of a building
    D. follows the Custodial Foreman through a building containing large, open areas

2. According to the passage above, the post assignment method is used MOSTLY where   2.____
   the buildings to be cleaned are _____ in size and situated _____.

    A. large; close together   B. small; close together
    C. large; far apart   D. small; far apart

3. As used in the passage above, the word *economical* means MOST NEARLY   3.____

    A. thrifty   B. agreed   C. unusual   D. wasteful

Questions 4-25.

DIRECTIONS: Each question consists of a statement. You are to indicate whether the statement is TRUE (T) or FALSE (F). *PRINT THE LETTER OF THE CORRECT ANSWER IN THE SPACE AT THE RIGHT.*

Questions 4-8.

DIRECTIONS: Questions 4 through 8 are to be answered in accordance with the information given in the following paragraph.

The removal of fine, loose dirt or dust from desks, chairs, filing cabinets, tables, and other furniture or office machines is called dusting. A yard of clean soft cloth, folded into a pad about nine inches square, is best for dusting. The cloth should be dry since oil or water on the cloth may streak the surface that is being dusted. When dusting a desk, care must be taken to put back in the same place any papers that were lifted or moved to one side. Thorough dusting of an office is important in order for the office to look neat and for the health of the people who work in that office.

4. The removal of fine, loose dirt or dust from furniture or office machines is called dusting.   4.____

5. A pad of cloth twelve inches square is best for dusting.   5.____

6. A dry cloth will streak the surface that is being dusted.   6.____

7. Papers that have been lifted or moved to one side when dusting a desk should be put back in the same place.   7.____

8. It is not important to dust an office thoroughly.   8.____

Questions 9-18.

DIRECTIONS: Questions 9 through 18 are to be answered in accordance with the information given in the following paragraphs.

WASHING OF WALLS

The washing of walls is important since wall-cleaning costs are an expensive item in the operating cost of building maintenance.

There is a right and a wrong way to wash walls. Streaks may be caused by water running down the dry wall below the place where one is working. This can be prevented by first wetting a section of the wall with water, starting at the bottom and working up before starting the actual washing operation with cleaning solution. Then, if the water runs down the wet wall, there will be almost no streaking. While washing a wall, the temperature should be reasonably low so that the water will not dry on the wall and cause streaks. Once the dirt on the wall is moistened, the wall must be kept wet until the dirt is removed. The washing of walls should be done with good sponges. One sponge should be for cleaning on the dirty wall and one for rinsing.

When working with the cleaning solution, start at the top of the wall and use a circular motion of the sponge and hand. Work across a given section first to the right and then to the left, and so on down to the base.

After the dirt has been removed, take clean, cool water and a clean sponge and go over the wall to be sure that it is perfectly clean and that no traces of the cleaning solution remain on the wall. Even clean water drying unevenly on a wall will cause slight streaks which become noticeable on the walls.

9. The amount of money spent to wash walls is a very small part in the expenses of running a building.   9.____

10. To prevent streaks when washing a wall, an employee should FIRST wet the wall, starting at the top and working down to the base of a wall. 10.____

11. If a wall is wet in the right way, there will be practically no streaks caused by water running down the wet wall. 11.____

12. If the walls are washed when the room is hot, streaks can be caused by water drying too quickly. 12.____

13. Once a dirty wall is made wet with water, it should be dried completely before the dirt is removed. 13.____

14. To wash walls properly, an employee should use at least two good sponges. 14.____

15. When washing with the cleaning solution, start at the bottom of the wall and work to the top, using a circular motion of the hand and sponge. 15.____

16. When washing with the cleaning solution, the CORRECT method is to work across each part of the wall going first to the left and ending on the right. 16.____

17. After the wall has been washed with the cleaning solution, it must be gone over again with clean water to remove any solution which is left on the wall. 17.____

18. When clean water is used to wash a wall, streaks will never appear, even if the wall dries unevenly. 18.____

Questions 19-25.

DIRECTIONS: Questions 19 through 25 are to be answered in accordance with the information given in the following passage.

CLEANING ELECTRIC LIGHT FIXTURES

A room may be dark not because there are not enough light fixtures but because the globes are dirty. As frequently as found necessary, and at least once a year, each globe on a light fixture should be taken down and carefully washed. It should be cleaned by using a solution of warm water to which has been added about two tablespoons full of washing soda for each 10 quarts of water. The globe must be thoroughly dried before it is put back or it is liable to crack from the heat of the lamp. At the time the globe is washed, the metal parts of the fixture should be wiped with a rag dampened in plain warm water. Most metal fixtures have been lacquered, and any cleaning solution would tend to destroy the lacquer. The electric light bulb should be unscrewed from the fixture and wiped with a slighly damp cloth. If it is burned out, it should be replaced at this time.

19. Dirty light globes will reduce the amount of light in a room. 19.____

20. Light globes should be cleaned only when the attendant replaces a burned out light bulb in a fixture. 20.____

21. To clean light globes, a solution of cold water and ordinary household ammonia should be used. 21.____

22. If a light globe is not completely dry when it is put back on a fixture after washing, the heat from the light bulb can break the globe.   22._____

23. The metal parts of a light fixture should be cleaned by using a dry rag to which has been added a few drops of a cleaning solution.   23._____

24. Most metal light fixtures have a coating of lacquer on them.   24._____

25. To clean a light bulb in a fixture, it should be unscrewed and wiped with a damp cloth.   25._____

KEY (CORRECT ANSWERS)

1.	C	11.	T
2.	D	12.	T
3.	A	13.	F
4.	T	14.	T
5.	F	15.	F
6.	F	16.	F
7.	T	17.	T
8.	F	18.	F
9.	F	19.	T
10.	F	20.	F

21. F
22. T
23. F
24. T
25. T

PREPARING WRITTEN MATERIAL

PARAGRAPH REARRANGEMENT
COMMENTARY

The sentences that follow are in scrambled order. You are to rearrange them in proper order and indicate the letter choice containing the correct answer at the space at the right.

Each group of sentences in this section is actually a paragraph presented in scrambled order. Each sentence in the group has a place in that paragraph; no sentence is to be left out. You are to read each group of sentences and decide upon the best order in which to put the sentences so as to form a well-organized paragraph.

The questions in this section measure the ability to solve a problem when all the facts relevant to its solution are not given.

More specifically, certain positions of responsibility and authority require the employee to discover connection between events sometimes, apparently, unrelated. In order to do this, the employee will find it necessary to correctly infer that unspecified events have probably occurred or are likely to occur. This ability becomes especially important when action must be taken on incomplete information.

Accordingly, these questions require competitors to choose among several suggested alternatives, each of which presents a different sequential arrangement of the events. Competitors must choose the MOST logical of the suggested sequences.

In order to do so, they may be required to draw on general knowledge to infer missing concepts or events that are essential to sequencing the given events. Competitors should be careful to infer only what is essential to the sequence. The plausibility of the wrong alternatives will always require the inclusion of unlikely events or of additional chains of events which are NOT essential to sequencing the given events.

It's very important to remember that you are looking for the best of the four possible choices, and that the best choice of all may not even be one of the answers you're given to choose from.

There is no one right way to solve these problems. Many people have found it helpful to first write out the order of the sentences, as they would have arranged them, on their scrap paper before looking at the possible answers. If their optimum answer is there, this can save them some time. If it isn't, this method can still give insight into solving the problem. Others find it most helpful to just go through each of the possible choices, contrasting each as they go along. You should use whatever method feels comfortable and works for you.

While most of these types of questions are not that difficult, we've added a higher percentage of the difficult type, just to give you more practice. Usually there are only one or two questions on this section that contain such subtle distinctions that you're unable to answer confidently. And you then may find yourself stuck deciding between two possible choices, neither of which you're sure about.

EXAMINATION SECTION

TEST 1

DIRECTIONS: The following groups of sentences need to be arranged in an order that makes sense. Select the letter preceding the sequence that represents the BEST sentence order. *PRINT THE LETTER OF THE CORRECT ANSWER IN THE SPACE AT THE RIGHT.*

1. I. The keyboard was purposely designed to be a little awkward to slow typists down.
    II. The arrangement of letters on the keyboard of a typewriter was not designed for the convenience of the typist.
    III. Fortunately, no one is suggesting that a new keyboard be designed right away.
    IV. If one were, we would have to learn to type all over again.
    V. The reason was that the early machines were slower than the typists and would jam easily.
    The CORRECT answer is:
    A. I, III, IV, II, V
    B. II, V, I, IV, III
    C. V, I, II, III, IV
    D. II, I, V, III, IV

2. I. The majority of the new service jobs are part-time or low-paying.
    II. According to the U.S. Bureau of Labor Statistics, jobs in the service sector constitute 72% of all jobs in this country.
    III. If more and more workers receive less and less money, who will buy the goods and services needed to keep the economy going?
    IV. The service sector is by far the fastest growing part of the United States economy.
    V. Some economists look upon this trend with great concern.
    The CORRECT answer is:
    A. II, IV, I, V, III
    B. II, III, IV, I, V
    C. V, IV, II, III, I
    D. III, I, II, IV, V

3. I. They can also affect one's endurance.
    II. This can stabilize blood sugar levels, and ensure that the brain is receiving a steady, constant, supply of glucose, so that one is *hitting on all cylinders* while taking the test.
    III. By food, we mean real food, not junk food or unhealthy snacks.
    IV. For this reason, it is important not to skip a meal, and to bring food with you to the exam.
    V. One's blood sugar levels can affect how clearly one is able to think and concentrate during an exam.
    The CORRECT answer is:
    A. V, IV, II, III, I
    B. V, II, I, IV, III
    C. V, I, IV, III, II
    D. V, IV, I, III, II

4. I. Those who are the embodiment of desire are absorbed in material quests, and those who are the embodiment of feeling are warriors who value power more than possession.
    II. These qualities are in everyone, but in different degrees.
    III. But those who value understanding yearn not for goods or victory, but for knowledge.
    IV. According to Plato, human behavior flows from three main sources: desire, emotion, and knowledge.
    V. In the perfect state, the industrial forces would produce but not rule, the military would protect but not rule, and the forces of knowledge, the philosopher kings, would reign.
    The CORRECT answer is:
    A. IV, V, I, II, III   B. V, I, II, III, IV
    C. IV, III, II, I, V   D. IV, II, I, III, V

4.____

5. I. Of the more than 26,000 tons of garbage produced daily in New York City, 12,000 tons arrive daily at Fresh Kills.
    II. In a month, enough garbage accumulates there to fill the Empire State Building.
    III. In 1937, the Supreme Court halted the practice of dumping the trash of New York City into the sea.
    IV. Although the garbage is compacted, in a few years the mounds of garbage at Fresh Kills will be the highest points south of Maine's Mount Desert Island on the Eastern Seaboard.
    V. Instead, tugboats now pull barges of much of the trash to Staten Island and the largest landfill in the world, Fresh Kills.
    The CORRECT answer is:
    A. III, V, IV, I, II   B. III, V, II, IV, I
    C. III, V, I, II, IV   D. III, II, V, IV, I

5.____

6. I. Communists rank equality very high, but freedom very low.
    II. Unlike communists, conservatives place a high value on freedom and a very low value on equality.
    III. A recent study demonstrated that one way to classify people's political beliefs is to look at the importance placed on two words: freedom and equality.
    IV. Thus, by demonstrating how members of these groups feel about the two words, the study has proved to be useful for political analysts in several European countries.
    V. According to the study, socialists and liberals rank both freedom and equality very high, while fascists rate both very low.
    The CORRECT answer is:
    A. III, V, I, II, IV   B. V, IV, III, I, II
    C. III, V, IV, II, I   D. III, I, II, IV, V

6.____

7. I. "Can there be anything more amazing than this?"
    II. If the riddle is successfully answered, his dead brothers will be brought back to life.
    III. "Even though man sees those around him dying every day," says Dharmaraj, "he still believes and acts as if he were immortal."
    IV. "What is the cause of ceaseless wonder?" asks the Lord of the Lake.
    V. In the ancient epic, The Mahabharata, a riddle is asked of one of the Pandava brothers.
    The CORRECT answer is:
    A. V, II, I, IV, III
    B. V, IV, III, I, II
    C. V, II, IV, III, I
    D. V, II, IV, I, III

8. I. On the contrary, the two main theories—the cooperative (neoclassical) theory and the radical (labor theory)—clearly rest on very different assumptions, which have very different ethical overtones.
    II. The distribution of income is the primary factor in determining the relative levels of material well-being that different groups or individuals attain.
    III. Of all issues in economics, the distribution of income is one of the most controversial.
    IV. The neoclassical theory tends to support the existing income distribution (or minor changes), while the labor theory ends to support substantial changes in the way income is distributed.
    V. The intensity of the controversy reflects the fact that different economic theories are not purely neutral, *detached* theories with no ethical or moral implications.
    The CORRECT answer is:
    A. II, I, V, IV, III
    B. III, II, V, I, IV
    C. III, V, II, I, IV
    D. III, V, IV, I, II

9. I. The pool acts as a broker and ensures that the cheapest power gets used first.
    II. Every six seconds, the pool's computer monitors all of the generating stations in the state and decides which to ask for more power and which to cut back.
    III. The buying and selling of electrical power is handled by the New York Power Pool in Guilderland, New York.
    IV. This is to the advantage of both the buying and selling utilities.
    V. The pool began operation in 1970, and consists of the state's eight electric utilities.
    The CORRECT answer is:
    A. V, I, II, III, IV
    B. IV, II, I, III, V
    C. III, V, I, IV, II
    D. V, III, IV, II, I

10. I. Modern English is much simpler grammatically than Old English.
    II. Finnish grammar is very complicated; there are some fifteen cases, for example.
    III. Chinese, a very old language, may seem to be the exception, but it is the great number of characters/words that must be mastered that makes it so difficult to learn, not its grammar.
    IV. The newest literary language—that is, written as well as spoken—is Finish, whose literary roots go back only to about the middle of the nineteenth century.
    V. Contrary to popular belief, the longer a language is been in use the simpler its grammar—not the reverse.
    The CORRECT answer is:
    A. IV, I, II, III, V
    B. V, I, IV, II, III
    C. I, II, IV, III, V
    D. IV, II, III, I, V

KEY (CORRECT ANSWERS)

1.	D	6.	A
2.	A	7.	C
3.	C	8.	B
4.	D	9.	C
5.	C	10.	B

TEST 2

DIRECTIONS: This type of question tests your ability to recognize accurate paraphrasing, well-constructed paragraphs, and appropriate style and tone. It is important that the answer you select contains only the facts or concepts given in the original sentences. It is also important that you be aware of incomplete sentences, inappropriate transitions, unsupported opinions, incorrect usage, and illogical sentence order. Paragraphs that do not include all the necessary facts and concepts, that distort them, or that add new ones are not considered correct.

The format for this section may vary. Sometimes, long paragraphs are given, and emphasis is placed on style and organization. Our first five questions are of this type. Other times, the paragraphs are shorter, and there is less emphasis on style and more emphasis on accurate representation of information. Our second group of five questions are of this nature.

For each of Questions 1 through 10, select the paragraph that BEST expresses the ideas contained in the sentences above it. *PRINT THE LETTER OF THE CORRECT ANSWER IN THE SPACE AT THE RIGHT.*

1. I. Listening skills are very important for managers.
    II. Listening skills are not usually emphasized.
    III. Whenever managers are depicted in books, manuals or the media, they are always talking, never listening.
    IV. We'd like you to read the enclosed handout on listening skills and to try to consciously apply them this week.
    V. We guarantee they will improve the quality of your interactions.

    A. Unfortunately, listening skills are not usually emphasized for managers. Managers are always depicted as talking, never listening. We'd like you to read the enclosed handout on listening skills. Please try to apply these principles this week. If you do, we guarantee they will improve the quality of your interactions.
    B. The enclosed handout on listening skills will be important improving the quality of your interactions. We guarantee it. All you have to do is take sometime this week to read and to consciously try to apply the principles. Listening skills are very important for manages, but they are not usually emphasized. Whenever managers are depicted in books, manuals or the media, they are always talking, never listening.
    C. Listening well is one of the most important skills a manager can have, yet it's not usually given much attention. Think about any representation of managers in books, manuals, or in the media that you may have seen. They're always talking, never listening. We'd like you to read the enclosed handout on listening skills and consciously try to apply them the rest of the week. We guarantee you will see a difference in the quality of your interactions.

1.____

D. Effective listening, one very important tool in the effective manager's arsenal, is usually not emphasized enough. The usual depiction of managers in books, manuals or the media is one in which they are always talking, never listening. We'd like you to read the enclosed handout and consciously try to apply the information contained therein throughout the rest of the week. We feel sure that you will see a marked difference in the quality of your interactions.

2. I. Chekhov wrote three dramatic masterpieces which share certain themes and formats: <u>Uncle Vanya</u>, <u>The Cherry Orchard</u>, and <u>The Three Sisters</u>.
   II. They are primarily concerned with the passage of time and how this erodes human aspirations.
   III. The plays are haunted by the ghosts of the wasted life.
   IV. The characters are concerned with life's lesser problems; however, such as the inability to make decisions, loyalty to the wrong cause, and the inability to be clear.
   V. This results in sweet, almost aching, type of a sadness referred to as Chekhovian.

2.____

   A. Chekhov wrote three dramatic masterpieces: <u>Uncle Vanya</u>, <u>The Cherry Orchard</u>, and <u>The Three Sisters</u>. These masterpieces share certain themes and formats: the passage of time, how time erodes human aspirations, and the ghosts of wasted life. Each masterpiece is characterized by a sweet, almost aching, type of sadness that has become known as Chekhovian. The sweetness of this sadness hinges on the fact that it is not the great tragedies of life which are destroying these characters, but their minor flaws: indecisiveness, misplaced loyalty, unclarity.
   B. <u>The Cherry Orchard</u>, <u>Uncle Vanya</u>, and <u>The Three Sisters</u> are three dramatic masterpieces written by Chekhov that use similar formats to explore a common theme. Each is primarily concerned with the way that passing time wears down human aspirations, and each is haunted by the ghosts of the wasted life. The characters are shown struggling futilely with the lesser problems of life: indecisiveness, loyalty to the wrong cause, and the inability to be clear. These struggles create a mood of sweet, almost aching, sadness that has become known as Chekhovian.
   C. Chekhov's dramatic masterpieces are, along with <u>The Cherry Orchard</u>, <u>Uncle Vanya</u>, and <u>The Three Sisters</u>. These plays share certain thematic and formal similarities. They are concerned most of all with the passage of time and the way in which time erodes human aspirations. Each play is haunted by the specter of the wasted life. Chekhov's characters are caught, however, by life's lesser snares: indecisiveness, loyalty to the wrong cause, and unclarity. The characteristic mood is a sweet, almost aching type of sadness that has come to be known as Chekhovian.
   D. A Chekhovian mood is characterized by sweet, almost aching, sadness. The term comes from three dramatic tragedies by Chekhov which revolve around the sadness of a wasted life. The three masterpieces (<u>Uncle Vanya</u>, <u>The Three Sisters</u>, and <u>The Cherry Orchard</u>) share the same

theme and format. The plays are concerned with how the passage of time erodes human aspirations. They are peopled with characters who are struggling with life's lesser problems. These are people who are indecisive, loyal to the wrong causes, or are unable to make themselves clear.

3.
  I. Movie previews have often helped producers decide which parts of movies they should take out or leave in.
  II. The first 1933 preview of King Kong was very helpful to the producers because many people ran screaming from the theater and would not return when four men first attacked by Kong were eaten by giant spiders.
  III. The 1950 premiere of Sunset Boulevard resulted in the filming of an entirely new beginning, and a delay of six months in the film's release.
  IV. In the original opening scene, William Holden was in a morgue talking with thirty-six other "corpses" about the ways some of them had died.
  V. When he began to tell them of his life with Gloria Swanson, the audience found this hilarious, instead of taking the scene seriously.

3.____

  A. Movie previews have often helped producers decide what parts of movies they should leave in or take out. For example, the first preview of King Kong in 1933 was very helpful. In one scene, four men were first attacked by Kong and then eaten by giant spiders. Many members of the audience ran screaming from the theater and would not return. The premiere of the 1950 film Sunset Boulevard was also very helpful. In the original opening scene, William Holden was in a morgue with thirty-six other "corpses," discussing the ways some of them had died. When he began to tell them of his life with Gloria Swanson, the audience found this hilarious. They were supposed to take the scene seriously. The result was a delay of six months in the release of the film while a new beginning was added.
  B. Movie previews have often helped producers decide whether they should change various parts of a movie. After the 1933 preview of King Kong, a scene in which four men who had been attacked by Kong were eaten by giant spiders was taken out as many people ran screaming from the theater and would not return. The 1950 premiere of Sunset Boulevard also led to some changes. In the original opening scene, William Holden was in a morgue talking with thirty-six other "corpses" about the ways some of them had died. When he began to tell them of his life with Gloria Swanson, the audience found this hilarious, instead of taking the scene seriously.
  C. What do Sunset Boulevard and King Kong have in common? Both show the value of using movie previews to test audience reaction. The first 1933 preview of King Kong showed that a scene showing four men being eaten by giant spiders after having been attacked by Kong was too frightening for many people. They ran screaming from the theater and couldn't be coaxed back. The 1950 premiere of Sunset Boulevard was also a scream, but not the kind the producers intended. The movie opens

with William Holden lying in a morgue discussing the ways they had died with thirty-six other "corpses." When he began to tell them of his life with Gloria Swanson, the audience couldn't take him seriously. Their laughter caused a six-month delay while the beginning was rewritten.

D. Producers very often use movie previews to decide if changes are needed. The premiere of Sunset Boulevard in 1950 led to a new beginning and a six-month delay in film release. At the beginning, William Holden and thirty-six other "corpses" discuss the ways some of them died. Rather than taking this seriously, the audience thought it was hilarious when he began to tell them of his life with Gloria Swanson. The first 1933 preview of King Kong was very helpful for its producers because one scene so terrified the audience that many of them ran screaming from the theater and would not return. In this particular scene, four men who had first been attacked by Kong were eaten by giant spiders.

4. I. It is common for supervisors to view employees as "things" to be manipulated. 4.____
    II. This approach does not motivate employees, nor does the carrot-and-stick approach because employees often recognize these behaviors and resent them.
    III. Supervisors can change these behaviors by using self-inquiry and persistence.
    IV. The best managers genuinely respect those they work with, are supportive and helpful, and are interested in working as a team with those they supervise.
    V. They disagree with the Golden Rule that says "he or she who has the gold makes the rules."

    A. Some managers act as if they think the Golden Rule means "he or she who has the gold makes the rules." They show disrespect to employees by seeing them as "things" to be manipulated. Obviously, this approach does not motivate employees any more than the carrot-and-stick approach motivates them. The employees are smart enough to spot these behaviors and resent them. On the other hand, the managers genuinely respect those they work with, are supportive and helpful, and are interested in working as a team. Self-inquiry and persistence can change even the former type of supervisor into the latter.
    B. Many supervisors all into the trap of viewing employees as "things" to be manipulated, or try to motivate them by using a carrot-and-stick approach. These methods do not motivate employees, who often recognize the behaviors and resent them. Supervisors can change these behaviors, however, by using self-inquiry and persistence. The best managers are supportive and helpful, and have genuine respect for those with whom they work. They are interested in working as a team with those they supervise. To them, the Golden Rule is not "he or she who has the gold makes the rules."
    C. Some supervisors see employees as "things" to be used or manipulated using a carrot-and-stick technique. These methods don't work. Employees often see through them and resent them. A supervisor who

wants to change may do so. The techniques of self-inquiry and persistence can be used to turn him or her into the type of supervisor who doesn't think the Golden Rule is "he or she who has the gold makes the rules." They may become like the best managers who treat those with whom they work with respect and give them help and support. These are the manager who know how to build a team.

D. Unfortunately, many supervisors act as if their employees are objects whose movements they can position at will. This mistaken belief has the same result as another popular motivational technique—the carrot-and-stick approach. Both attitudes can lead to the same result—resentment from those employees who recognize the behaviors for what they are. Supervisors who recognize these behaviors can change through the use of persistence and the use of self-inquiry. It's important to remember that the best managers respect their employees. They readily give necessary help and support and are interested in working as a team with those they supervise. To these managers, the Golden Rule is not "he or she who has the gold makes the rules."

5.
I. The first half of the nineteenth century produced a group of pessimistic poets—Byron, De Musset, Heine, Pushkin, and Leopardi.
II. It also produced a group of pessimistic composers—Schubert, Chopin, Schumann, and even the later Beethoven.
III. Above all, in philosophy, there was the profoundly pessimistic philosopher, Schopenhauer.
IV. The Revolution was dead, the Bourbons were restored, the feudal barons were reclaiming their land, and progress everywhere was being suppressed, as the great age was over.
V. "I thank God," said Goethe, "that I am not young in so thoroughly finished a world."

   A. "I thank God," said Goethe, "that I am not young in so thoroughly finished a world." The Revolution was dead, the Bourbons were restored, the feudal barons were reclaiming their land, and progress everywhere was being suppressed. The first half of the nineteenth century produced a group of pessimistic poets: Byron, De Musset, Heine, Pushkin, and Leopardi. It also produced pessimistic composers: Schubert, Chopin, Schumann. Although Beethoven came later, he fits into this group, too. Finally and above all, it also produced a profoundly pessimistic philosopher, Schopenhauer. The great age was over.

   B. The first half of the nineteenth century produced a group of pessimistic poets: Byron, De Musset, Heine, Pushkin, and Leopardi. It produced a group of pessimistic composers: Schubert, Chopin, Schumann, and even the later Beethoven. Above all, it produced a profoundly pessimistic philosopher, Schopenhauer. For each of these men, the great age was over. The Revolution was dead, and the Bourbons were restored. The feudal barons were reclaiming their land, and progress everywhere was being suppressed.

C. The great age was over. The Revolution was dead—the Bourbons were restored, and the feudal barons were reclaiming their land. Progress everywhere was being suppressed. Out of this climate came a profound pessimism. Poets, like Byron, De Musset, Heine, Pushkin, and Leopardi; composers, like Schubert, Chopin, Schumann, and even the later Beethoven; and above all, a profoundly pessimistic philosopher, Schopenauer. This pessimism which arose in the first half of the nineteenth century is illustrated by these words of Goethe, "I thank God that I am not young in so thoroughly finished a world."

D. The first half of the nineteenth century produced a group of pessimistic poets, Byron, De Musset, Heine, Pushkin, and Leopardi—and a group of pessimistic composers, Schubert, Chopin, Schumann, and the later Beethoven. Above it all, it produced a profoundly pessimistic philosopher, Schopenhauer. The great age was over. The Revolution was dead, the Bourbons were restored, the feudal barons were reclaiming their land, and progress everywhere was being suppressed. "I thank God," said Goethe, "that I am not young in so thoroughly finished a world."

6.
I. A new manager sometimes may feel insecure about his or her competence in the new position.
II. The new manager may then exhibit defensive or arrogant behavior towards those one supervises, or the new manager may direct overly flattering behavior toward one's new supervisor.

   A. Sometimes, a new manager may feel insecure about his or her ability to perform well in this new position. The insecurity may lead him or her to treat others differently. He or she may display arrogant or defensive behavior towards those he or she supervises, or be overly flattering to his or her new supervisor.
   B. A new manager may sometimes feel insecure about his or her ability to perform well in the new position. He or she may then become arrogant, defensive, or overly flattering towards those he or she works with.
   C. There are times when a new manager may be insecure about how well he or she can perform in the new job. The new manager may also behave defensive or act in an arrogant way towards those he or she supervises, or overly flatter his or her boss.
   D. Sometimes a new manager may feel insecure about his or her ability to perform well in the new position. He or she may then display arrogant or defensive behavior towards those they supervise, or become overly flattering towards their supervisors.

6.____

7.
I. It is possible to eliminate unwanted behavior by bringing it under stimulus control—tying the behavior to a cue, and then never, or rarely, giving the cue.
II. One trainer successfully used this method to keep an energetic young porpoise from coming out of her tank whenever she felt like it, which was potentially dangerous.
III. Her trainer taught her to do it for a reward, in response to a hand signal, and then rarely gave the signal.

7.____

A. Unwanted behavior can be eliminated by tying the behavior to a cue, and then never, or rarely, giving the cue. This is called stimulus control. One trainer was able to use this method to keep an energetic young porpoise from coming out of her tank by teaching her to come out for a reward in response to a hand signal, and then rarely giving the signal.

B. Stimulus control can be used to eliminate unwanted behavior. In this method, behavior is tied to a cue, and then the cue is rarely, if ever, given. One trainer was able to successfully use stimulus control to keep an energetic young porpoise from coming out of her tank whenever she felt like it—a potentially dangerous practice. She taught the porpoise to come out for a reward when she gave a hand signal, and then rarely gave the signal.

C. It is possible to eliminate behavior that is undesirable by bringing it under stimulus control by tying behavior to a signal, and then rarely giving the signal. One trainer successfully used this method to keep an energetic porpoise from coming out of her tank, a potentially dangerous situation. Her trainer taught the porpoise to do it for a reward, in response to a hand signal, and then would rarely give the signal.

D. By using stimulus control, it is possible to eliminate unwanted behavior by tying the behavior to a cue, and then rarely or never give the cue. One trainer was able to use this method to successfully stop a young porpoise from coming out of her tank whenever she felt like it. To curb this potentially dangerous practice, the porpoise was taught by the trainer to come out of the tank for a reward, in response to a hand signal, and then rarely given the signal.

8. I. There is a great deal of concern over the safety of commercial trucks, caused by their greatly increased role in serious accidents since federal deregulation in 1981.
   II. Recently, 60 percent of trucks in New York and Connecticut and 70 percent of trucks in Maryland randomly stopped by state troopers failed safety inspections.
   III. Sixteen states in the United States require no training at all for truck drivers.

   A. Since federal deregulation in 1981, there has been a great deal of concern over the safety of commercial trucks, and their greatly increased role in serious accidents. Recently, 60 percent of trucks in New York and Connecticut, and 70 percent of trucks in Maryland failed safety inspections. Sixteen states in the United States require no training at all for truck drivers.
   B. There is a great deal of concern over the safety of commercial trucks since federal deregulation in 1981. Their role in serious accidents has greatly increased. Recently, 60 percent of trucks randomly stopped in Connecticut and New York and 70 percent in Maryland failed safety inspections conducted by state troopers. Sixteen states in the United States provide no training at all for truck drivers.
   C. Commercial trucks have a greatly increased role in serious accidents since federal deregulation in 1981. This has led to a great deal of concern.

Recently, 70 percent of trucks in Maryland and 60 percent of trucks in New York and Connecticut failed inspection of those that were randomly stopped by state troopers. Sixteen states in the United States require no training for all truck drivers.

D. Since federal deregulation in 1981, the role that commercial trucks have played in serious accidents has greatly increased, and this has led to a great deal of concern. Recently, 60 percent of trucks in New York and Connecticut, and 70 percent of trucks in Maryland randomly stopped by state troopers failed safety inspections. Sixteen states in the U.S. don't require any training for truck drivers.

9.
I. No matter how much some people have, they still feel unsatisfied and want more, or want to keep what they have forever.
II. One recent television documentary showed several people flying from New York to Paris for a one-day shopping spree to buy platinum earrings, because they were bored.
III. In Brazil, some people were ordering coffins that cost a minimum of $45,000 and are equipping them with deluxe stereos, televisions, and other graveyard necessities.

9.____

A. Some people, despite having a great deal, still feel unsatisfied and want more, or think they can keep what they have forever. One recent documentary on television showed several people enroute from Paris to New York for a one day shopping spree to buy platinum earrings, because they were bored. Some people in Brazil are even ordering coffins equipped with such graveyard necessities as deluxe stereos and televisions. The price of the coffins start at $45,000.
B. No matter how much some people have, they may feel unsatisfied. This leads them to want more, or to want to keep what they have forever. Recently, a television documentary depicting several people flying from New York to Paris for a one day shopping spree to buy platinum earrings. They were bored. Some people in Brazil are ordering coffins that cost at least $45,000 and come equipped with deluxe televisions, stereos and other necessary graveyard items.
C. Some people will be dissatisfied no matter how much they have. They may want more, or they may want to keep what they have forever. One recent television documentary showed several people, motivated by boredom, jetting from New York to Paris for a one-day shopping spree to buy platinum earrings. In Brazil, some people are ordering coffins equipped with deluxe stereos, televisions and other graveyard necessities. The minimum price for these coffins—$45,000.
D. Some people are never satisfied. No matter how much they have they still want more, or think they can keep what they have forever. One television documentary recently showed several people flying from New York to Paris for the day to buy platinum earrings because they were bored. In Brazil, some people are ordering coffins that cost $45,000 and are equipped with deluxe stereos, televisions and other graveyard necessities.

10. I. A television signal or video signal has three parts.
    II. Its parts are the black-and-white portion, the color portion, and the synchronizing (sync) pulses, which keep the picture stable.
    III. Each video source, whether it's a camera or a video-cassette recorder contains its own generator of these synchronizing pulses to accompany the picture that it's sending in order to keep it steady and straight.
    IV. In order to produce a clean recording, a video-cassette recorder must "lock-up" to the sync pulses that are part of the video it is trying to record, and this effort may be very noticeable if the device does not have gunlock.

    A. There are three parts to a television or video signal: the black-and-white part, the color part, and the synchronizing (sync) pulses, which keep the picture stable. Whether it's a video-cassette recorder or a camera, each video source contains its own pulse that synchronizes and generates the picture it's sending in order to keep it straight and steady. A video-cassette recorder must "lock up" to the sync pulses that are part of the video it's trying to record. If the device doesn't have gunlock, this effort must be very noticeable.
    B. A video signal or television is comprised of three parts: the black-and-white portion, the color portion, and the sync (synchronizing) pulses, which keep the picture stable. Whether it's a camera or a video-cassette recorder, each video source contains its own generator of these synchronizing pulses. These accompany the picture that it's sending in order to keep it straight and steady. A video-cassette recorder must "lock up" to the sync pulses that are part of the video it is trying to record in order to produce a clean recording. This effort may be very noticeable if the device does not have gunlock.
    C. There are three parts to a television or video signal: the color portion, the black-and-white portion, and the sync (synchronizing pulses). These keep the picture stable. Each video source, whether it's a video-cassette recorder or a camera, generates these synchronizing pulses accompanying the picture it's sending in order to keep it straight and steady. If a clean recording is to be produced, a video-cassette recorder must store the sync pulses that are part of the video it is trying to record. This effort may not be noticeable if the device does not have gunlock.
    D. A television signal or video signal has three parts: the black-and-white portion, the color portion, and the synchronizing (sync) pulses. It's the sync pulses which keep the picture stable, which accompany it and keep it steady and straight. Whether it's a camera or a video-cassette recorder, each video source contains its own generator of these synchronizing pulses. To produce a clean recording, a video-cassette recorder must "lock up" to the sync pulses that are part of the video it is trying to record. If the device does not have gunlock, this effort may be very noticeable.

10.____

KEY (CORRECT ANSWERS)

1. C
2. B
3. A
4. B
5. D
6. A
7. B
8. D
9. C
10. D

PREPARING WRITTEN MATERIAL
EXAMINATION SECTION
TEST 1

DIRECTIONS: Each of Questions 1 through 5 consists of a sentence which may or may not be an example of good formal English usage. Examine each sentence, considering grammar, punctuation, spelling, capitalization, and awkwardness. Then choose the correct statement about it from the four options below it. If the English usage in the sentence given is better than any of the changes suggested in options B, C, or D, pick option A. (Do not pick an option that will change the meaning of the sentence.) *PRINT THE LETTER OF THE CORRECT ANSWER IN THE SPACE AT THE RIGHT.*

1. I don't know who could possibly of broken it. 1.____
   A. This is an example of good formal English usage.
   B. The word "who" should be replaced by the word "whom."
   C. The word "of" should be replaced by the word "have."
   D. The word "broken" should be replaced by the word "broke."

2. Telephoning is easier than to write. 2.____
   A. This is an example of good formal English usage.
   B. The word "telephoning" should be spelled "telephoneing."
   C. The word "than" should be replaced by the word "then."
   D. The words "to write" should be replaced by the word "writing."

3. The two operators who have been assigned to these consoles are on vacation. 3.____
   A. This is an example of good formal English usage.
   B. A comma should be placed after the word "operators."
   C. The word "who" should be replaced by the word "whom."
   D. The word "are" should be replaced by the word "is."

4. You were suppose to teach mc how to operate a plugboard. 4.____
   A. This is an example of good formal English usage.
   B. The word "were" should be replaced by the word "was."
   C. The word "suppose" should be replaced by the word "supposed."
   D. The word "teach" should be replaced by the word "learn."

5. If you had taken my advice; you would have spoken with him. 5.____
   A. This is an example of good formal English usage.
   B. The word "advice" should be spelled "advise."
   C. The words "had taken" should be replaced by the word "take."
   D. The semicolon should be changed to a comma.

KEY (CORRECT ANSWERS)

1. C
2. D
3. A
4. C
5. D

TEST 2

DIRECTIONS: Select the correct answer. *PRINT THE LETTER OF THE CORRECT ANSWER IN THE SPACE AT THE RIGHT.*

1. The one of the following sentences which is MOST acceptable from the viewpoint of correct grammatical usage is:
    A. I do not know which action will have worser results.
    B. He should of known better.
    C. Both the officer on the scene, and his immediate supervisor, is charged with the responsibility.
    D. An officer must have initiative because his supervisor will not always be available to answer questions.

    1.____

2. The one of the following sentences which is MOST acceptable from the viewpoint of correct grammatical usage is:
    A. Of all the officers available, the better one for the job will be picked.
    B. Strict orders were given to all the officers, except he.
    C. Study of the law will enable you to perform your duties more efficiently.
    D. It seems to me that you was wrong in failing to search the two men.

    2.____

3. The one of the following sentences which does NOT contain a misspelled word is:
    A. The duties you will perform are similar to the duties of a patrolman.
    B. Officers must be constantly alert to sieze the initiative.
    C. Officers in this organization are not entitled to special privileges.
    D. Any changes in procedure will be announced publically.

    3.____

4. The one of the following sentences which does NOT contain a misspelled word is:
    A. It will be to your advantage to keep your firearm in good working condition.
    B. There are approximately fourty men on sick leave.
    C. Your first duty will be to pursuade the person to obey the law.
    D. Fires often begin in flameable material kept in lockers.

    4.____

5. The one of the following sentences which does NOT contain a misspelled word is:
    A. Offices are not required to perform technical maintanance.
    B. He violated the regulations on two occasions.
    C. Every employee will be held responable for errors.
    D. This was his nineth absence in a year.

    5.____

KEY (CORRECT ANSWERS)

1. D
2. C
3. C
4. A
5. B

TEST 3

DIRECTIONS: Select the correct answer. *PRINT THE LETTER OF THE CORRECT ANSWER IN THE SPACE AT THE RIGHT.*

1. You are answering a letter that was written on the letterhead of the ABC Company and signed by James H. Wood, Treasurer.
   What is usually considered to be the correct salutation to use in your reply?
   A. Dear ABC Company:
   B. Dear Sirs:
   C. Dear Mr. Wood:
   D. Dear Mr. Treasurer:

   1.____

2. Assume that one of your duties is to handle routine letters of inquiry from the public.
   The one of the following which is usually considered to be MOST desirable in replying to such a letter is a
   A. detailed answer handwritten on the original letter of inquiry
   B. phone call, since you can cover details more easily over the phone than in a letter
   C. short letter giving the specific information requested
   D. long letter discussing all possible aspects of the question raised

   2.____

3. The CHIEF reason for dividing a letter into paragraphs is to
   A. make the message clear to the reader by starting a new paragraph for each new topic
   B. make a short letter occupy as much of the page as possible
   C. keep the reader's attention by providing a pause from time to time
   D. make the letter look neat and businesslike

   3.____

4. Your superior has asked you to send an e-mail from your agency to a government agency in another city. He has written out the message and has indicated the name of the government agency.
   When you dictate the message to your secretary, which of the following items that your superior has NOT mentioned must you be sure to include?
   A. Today's date
   B. The full address of the government agency
   C. A polite opening such as "Dear Sirs"
   D. A final sentence such as "We would appreciate hearing from your agency in reply as soon as is convenient for you"

   4.____

5. The one of the following sentences which is grammatically preferable to the others is:
   A. Our engineers will go over your blueprints so that you may have no problems in construction.
   B. For a long time he had been arguing that we, not he, are to blame for the confusion.
   C. I worked on this automobile for two hours and still cannot find out what is wrong with it.
   D. Accustomed to all kinds of hardships, fatigue seldom bothers veteran policemen.

   5.____

KEY (CORRECT ANSWERS)

1. C
2. C
3. A
4. B
5. A

TEST 4

DIRECTIONS: Select the correct answer. *PRINT THE LETTER OF THE CORRECT ANSWER IN THE SPACE AT THE RIGHT.*

1. Suppose that an applicant for a job as snow laborer presents a letter from a former employer stating: "John Smith has a pleasing manner and never got into an argument with his fellow employees. He was never late or absent." This letter
    A. indicates that with some training Smith will make a good snow gang boss
    B. presents no definite evidence of Smith's ability to do snow work
    C. proves definitely that Smith has never done any snow work before
    D. proves definitely that Smith will do better than average work as a snow laborer

   1.____

2. Suppose you must write a letter to a local organization in your section refusing a request in connection with collection of their refuse.
   You should start the letter by
    A. explaining in detail the consideration you gave the request
    B. praising the organization for its service to the community
    C. quoting the regulation which forbids granting the request
    D. stating your regret that the request cannot be granted

   2.____

3. Suppose a citizen writes in for information as to whether or not he may sweep refuse into the gutter. A Sanitation officer answers as follows:
   Dear Sir:
      No person is permitted to litter, sweep, throw or cast, or direct, suffer or permit any person under his control to litter, sweep, throw or cast any ashes, garbage, paper, dust, or other rubbish or refuse into any public street or place, vacant lot, air shaft, areaway, backyard or court.
                                   Very truly yours,
                                   John Doe
   This letter is *poorly* written CHIEFLY because
    A. the opening is not indented   B. the thought is not clear
    C. the tone is too formal and cold   D. there are too many commas used

   3.____

4. A section of a disciplinary report written by a Sanitation officer states: "It is requested that subject Sanitation man be advised that his future activities be directed towards reducing his recurrent tardiness else disciplinary action will be initiated which may result in summary discharge."
   This section of the report is *poorly* written MAINLY because
    A. at least one word is misspelled   B. it is not simply expressed
    C. more than one idea is expressed   D. the purpose is not stated

   4.____

5. A section of a disciplinary report written by an officer states: "He comes in late. He takes too much time for lunch. He is lazy. I recommend his services be dispensed with."
   This section of the report is *poorly* written MAINLY because
    A. it ends with a preposition   B. it is not well organized
    C. no supporting facts are stated   D. the sentences are too simple

   5.____

KEY (CORRECT ANSWERS)

1. B
2. D
3. C
4. B
5. C

BASIC CLEANING PROCEDURES

TABLE OF CONTENTS

		Page
I.	TRASH REMOVAL	1
II.	CLEANING URNS AND ASHTRAYS	3
III.	DUSTING	4
IV.	FLOOR DUSTING	12
V.	VACUUMING (WET, DAMP, SPOT)	14
VI.	MOPPING (WET, DAMP, SPOT)	16

BASIC CLEANING PROCEDURES

I. TRASH REMOVAL

PURPOSE: To remove waste from patient and tenant areas in order to provide the highest standard of sanitation; protection against fire, pests, odor, bacteria, and other health hazards; and for esthetic reasons.

EQUIPMENT:
    Utility cart
    Trash chart
    Bucket
    Germicidal detergent
    Plastic liners (small and large)
    Cloths
    Gloves
    Container for cigarette butts

SAFETY PRECAUTIONS:

1. Must wear gloves.

2. Never handle trash with bare hands.

3. Always empty cigarette butts into separate container that has water or sand in it.

4. If liners are not used, do not transfer trash from one container to another transfer trash into a liner.

5. Trash must be separated into two categories: General and Special, General

PROCEDURE

General

1. Assemble necessary equipment, prepare germicidal solution, and take to assigned area.

2. Put on gloves.

3. Pick up large trash on floor, place in trash container.

4. Close plastic liner and secure with tie.

5. Remove liner and place in trash bag on utility cart or place into trash cart, or other trash collection vehicle.

6. Emerge (dip) cloth into germicidal solution. Wring out thoroughly.

7. Wipe outside and inside of trash container. Dry with second cloth.

8. Replace liner. Liner should extend over top of trash container and fold outward over the upper rim. If plastic liners are not being used, use the Replacement Method—a clean container is exchanged for the dirty one.

9. Proceed with this procedure until all trash is collected or containers are full.

10. Place in utility room or an appropriate storage area until time for disposal.

11. Remove trash from the storage area at the end of the day or at some specified time (by cart or dolly) to dumpsters.

12. If large G.I. cans are used in the specified trash storage area, maintain as listed above.

13. At least once a month, take all trash cans to a specified area and thoroughly wash or steam clean.

14. If using the Replacement Method, dirty trash containers must be washed or steam-cleaned daily. Must be stored in inverted or upside-down position to air dry.

15. Clean all equipment and return to designated storage area. Restock utility cart.

Special Waste Handling Syringes-Hypodermic Needles-Razor Blades

1. Collect from specified areas (full disposable containers designed for this waste.

2. Place in 20-gallon galvanized container in locked designated area.

3. Call Garage for pick-up and disposal when container is full (10).

Glass and Aerosol Cans

1. Collect from designated areas in marked metal containers.

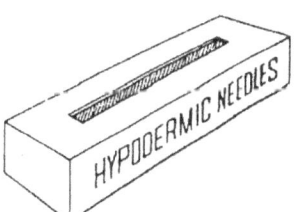

2. Place in 20-gallon galvanized containers in locked designated area daily.

3. Call Garage for pick-up and disposal when container is full.

Pathological Specimen (Tissue-flesh)

1. This type of waste is handled by a special technologist in the Hospital's Pathological Division.

2. Must be stored in refrigerator until incinerated.

3. Must be incinerated in special incinerator designed for this purpose.

Contaminated

The same procedure is used as for general collection with the following exceptions:

1. Must have covered step-on containers.

2. A second person is required to hold clean liner (top folded over hands for protection).

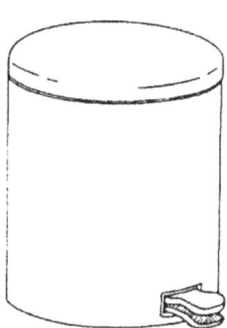

3. The tied soiled plastic liner is removed from the waste container and placed in a clean plastic liner and then deposited into the regular trash.

4. If in areas that are restricted, must wear protective garments.

II. CLEANING URNS AND ASHTRAYS

PURPOSE: To prevent fire hazards, to control bacteria, and for appearance.

EQUIPMENT:
- Utility cart
- Sifter or slit spoon
- Bucket for sand
- Cloths or sponges
- Container for cigarette butts
- Gloves
- Buckets (two)
- Counter brush and dustpans
- Germicidal detergent

SAFETY PRECAUTIONS:

1. Wear gloves.

2. Do not place plastic liners on inside of urns.

3. Sweep up all spilled sand immediately.

4. Make sure cigarette butts are placed in special container with water or sand in the bottom.

PROCEDURE

1. Assemble equipment. Prepare solution. Take to designated area.

2. Put on gloves.

3. Empty ashtrays into solution. Wash. Rinse in clear water. Dry. Return to proper area.

4. Make sure cigarette butts are placed in special container with water or sand in the bottom.

    a. Smoke stands and wall urns:

    (1) Empty cigarette butts into special container (by lifting out inside bucket or unscrewing base from top).

    (2) Wash, rinse, and dry the base, top, bucket and wall attachment.

    b. Floor urns with sand:

    (1) Take out large pieces of trash.

(2) Lift screen to remove cigarette butts and any other waste. Use sifter and spoon for this procedure if screens are not in use.

5. Replace sand if necessary. Sweep up any spilled sand.

6. Dip cloth into germicide solution. Wring out. Wipe off rim and outside of urns. Rinse and dry.

7. Continue this procedure until all urns are completed.

8. Clean all equipment and return to designated storage.

9. At least once a month collect cigarette receptacles. Take to utility room. Remove sand where applicable. Submerge in germicidal solution. Wash thoroughly. Rinse and dry. Replace sand and return to designated areas.

III. DUSTING

PURPOSE: To remove accumulated soil, to control bacteria, for protection, and for appearance.

EQUIPMENT:
    Utility cart
    Treated cloths
    Germicidal detergent
    Gloves
    Furniture polish
    Sweeping tool or broom
    Extension handle
    Clean cloths
    Buckets (two)
    Vacuum cleaner (Wet and Dry or Back Pack)
    Broom bags

SAFETY PRECAUTIONS:

1. A fold dust cloth is more efficient than a bunched cloth. When folded properly, cloth may have as many as 32 clean sides.

2. Use treated cloths or damp cloths when dusting. (Never use a feather duster.)

3. Oily cloths are fire hazards; they must be stored in a covered container.

4. Never shake cloth.

5. Never use circular motion. Dust with the grain.

6. Never use excessive water on wood furniture.

7. Do not take dust cloth from one patient unit to the next.

PROCEDURE

General – Dry

1. Assemble equipment. Prepare solution. Take to assigned area.

2. Put on gloves.

3. Fold treated cloth or damp germicidal cloth. (If using the damp germicidal cloth, use a second cloth for polishing.)

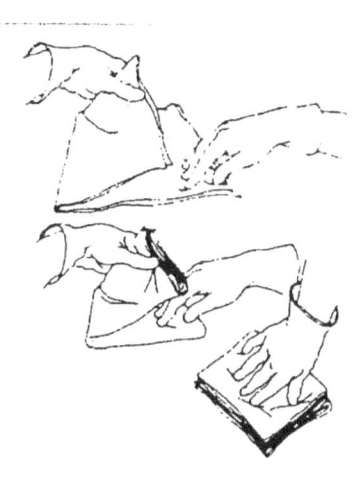

4. Look at area. Begin dusting at a point to avoid backtracking. Use both hands whenever possible. Begin with high furniture and work down to low furniture (for example, dust file cabinets before dusting desk tops).

5. Refold cloth when sides become dust filled or refresh by returning to germicidal solution.

6. Continue dusting until area is completed.

7. Inspect work.

8. Clean equipment and return to designated storage area. Cleaning cloths are placed in liner for laundering; woven treated paper dust cloths are discarded.

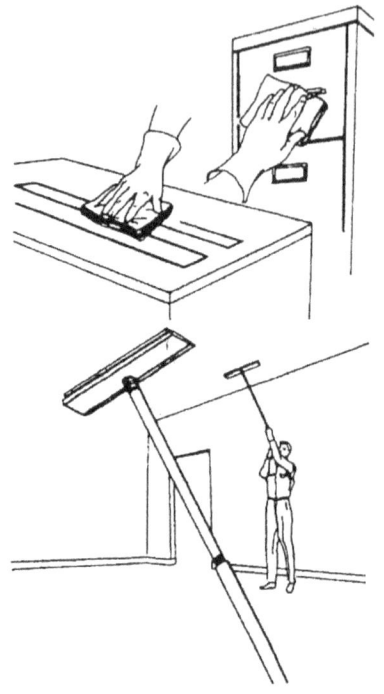

Wall and Ceiling Dusting

1. Assemble equipment. Take to assigned area.

2. Move furniture that will interfere with operation to one side of the room. Remove all pictures and other wall mountings and place in a safe area.

3. Put on gloves.

4. Dust ceiling. Start at back of room. Use vacuum or floor tool or covered broom with extension handle. Place dusting tool against ceiling surface and walk forward to the other end.

5. Turn and overlap stroke. Continue this procedure until completed.

6. Dust ceiling both cross-wise and lengthwise.

7. When ceiling is completed, dust walls from top to bottom. Use full-length vertical overlapping strokes. Include vents, ledges, and exposed pipes.

8. When one side of area is completed, replace furniture.

9. Move furniture from other side and continue the dusting procedure until entire area is completed.

10. Replace furniture, pictures, and other wall mountings.

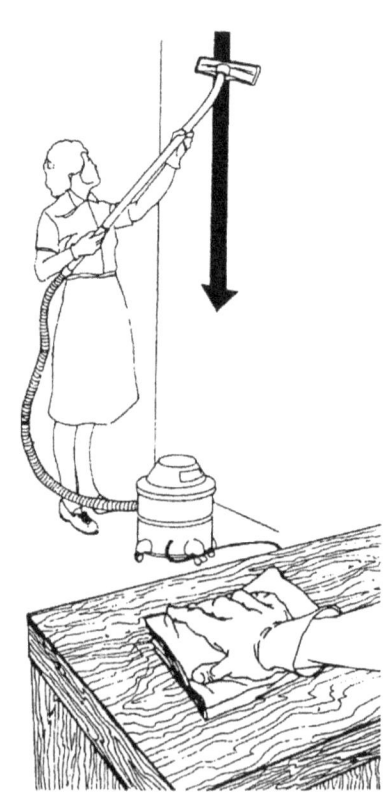

11. Inspect work.

12. Clean equipment. Return to designated storage areas. Broom bags are placed in plastic liner/bag for laundering; woven treated paper dust cloths are discarded.

General Comments for Dusting Different Types of Furniture

1. Wooden Furniture:

    a. Dust entire surface.

    b. Apply polish—pour small amount on damp cloth—rub with grain.

    c. Finish polishing by rubbing with dry cloth.

    d. Surface may be washed with natural detergent.

    CAUTION: Excessive amount of water should be avoided.

2. Metal Furniture:

    a. Dust entire surface.

    b. Surface may be washed and polished.

    c. Apply polish—pour small amount on damp cloth—rub in.

    d. Polish/rub thoroughly with a second cloth.

3. Plastic, Vinyl or Fiberglass:

    a. Dust entire area.

    b. Wash with germicidal cleaning solution.

    c. Rinse.

    d. Rub surface dry.

4. Leather:

    a. Damp dust.

    b. Clean with leather polish or saddle soap.

5. Upholstered Pieces:

   a. Vacuum entire surface thoroughly. Use push-pull strokes.

   b. Lift cushion—vacuum both sides, cushion support, and bottom of chair. Do not overlook corners and crevices.

   c. Check carefully for stains and report to supervisor.

6. Naugahyde:

   a. Elastic:

      (1) Ordinary Dirt: Ordinary dirt can be removed by washing with warm water and a mild soap. Apply soapy water to a large area and allow to soak for a few minutes. This will loosen the dirt. Brisk rubbing with a cloth should then remove most dirt. This procedure may be repeated several times if necessary.

      In the case of stubborn or imbedded dirt in the grain of the Naugahyde, a fingernail brush or other soft bristle brush may be used after the mild soap application has been made.

      If the dirt is extremely difficult to remove, wall washing preparations may be used. Abrasive cleaners may also be used. Abrasive cleaners should be used more cautiously and care exercised to prevent contact with the wood or metal parts of furniture or with any soft fabric which may be a part of the furniture.

      (2) Chewing Gum: Chewing gum may be removed by careful scraping and by applying kerosene, gasoline, or naphtha. If none of these are available, most hair oils or Three-In-One oil will soften the chewing gum so that it may be removed.

      (3) Tars, Asphalts, Creosote: Each of these items will stain Naugahyde if allowed to remain in contact. They should be wiped off

as quickly as possible and the area carefully cleaned with a cloth dampened with kerosene, range oil, gasoline, or naphtha.

(4) Paint: Paint should be removed immediately if possible. Do not use paint remover or liquid-type brush cleaners. An unprinted cloth dampened with kerosene, painter's naphtha or turpentine may be used. Care must be exercised to keep these fluids from contact with soft fabrics or with the wooden areas of the furniture.

(5) Sulphide Staining: Atmosphere permeated with coal gas or direct contact with hard-boiled eggs, "Cold Wave" solutions and other sulphide compounds can stain Naugahyde. These stains may be removed by placing a clean, unprinted piece of cloth over the spotted area and pouring a liberal amount of 6% hydrogen peroxide onto the cloth and allowing the saturated cloth to remain on the spotted area for at least thirty minutes to one hour. If spot is stubborn, allow the hydrogen peroxide saturated cloth to remain on the spotted area overnight. Caution must be used to see that the hydrogen peroxide solution does not come in contact with stained or lacquered wood and should not be allowed to seep into the seams as it will weaken the cotton thread.

(6) Nail Polish and Nail Polish Remover: These substances will cause permanent harm to Naugahyde on prolonged contact. Fast and careful wiping or blotting immediately after contact will minimize the staining. Spreading of the liquid while removing should be avoided.

(7) Shoe Polish: Most shoe polishes contain dyes which will penetrate the Naugahyde and stain it permanently. They should be wiped off as quickly as possible using kerosene, gasoline, naphtha, or lighter fluid. If staining occurs, the same procedure outlined above for sulphide staining using hydrogen peroxide should be tried.

(8) Shoe Heel Marks: Shoe heel marks can be removed by the same procedure as is recommended for paint.

(9) Ballpoint Ink: Ballpoint ink may sometimes removed if rubbed immediately with a damp cloth using water or rubbing alcohol. If this is not successful, the procedure outlined for sulphide staining may be tried.

(10) Generally, stains are found which do not respond to any of the other treatments. It is sometimes helpful to place the furniture in direct sunlight for two or three days. Mustard, ballpoint ink, certain shoe polishes and dyes will sometimes bleach out in direct sunlight and leave the Naugahyde undamaged.

(11) Waxing or Refinishing: Waxing improves the soil resistance and cleanability of Naugahyde, and any solid wax may be used.

b. Breathable: U.S. Naugaweave should be treated as a soft fabric and not as a fully vinyl-coated fabric. U.S. Naugaweave can be cleaned with foam-type cleansers generally used for soft fabrics.

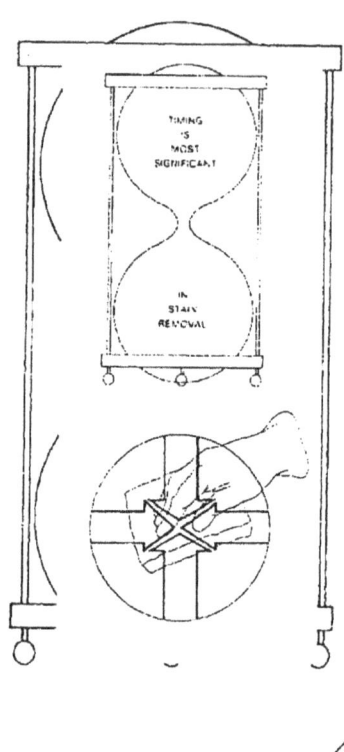

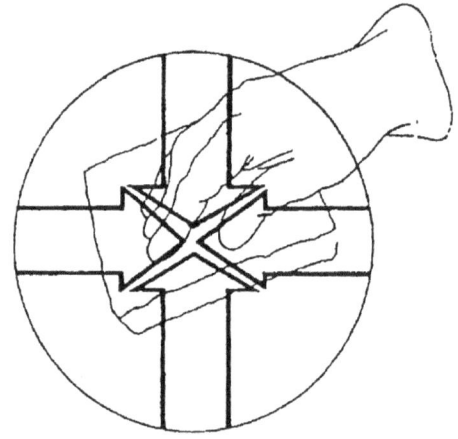

IV. FLOOR DUSTING
(Sweeping/Dusting with Covered Broom or Floor Tool with Chemically Treated Disposal Floor Cloth)

PURPOSE: To remove surface dirt, and make washing easier.

EQUIPMENT:
- Utility cart
- Dustpan
- Treated cloths, or
- Broom bags
- Counter brush
- Sweeping tool, or
- Vacuum cleaner

SAFETY PRECAUTIONS:

1. Never leave piles of dirt and trash in any area.

2. Lift sweeping tool at the end of each stroke. Do not tap.

3. Never put waste or sweepings in a patient's wastebasket.

4. Keep all equipment out of traffic areas.

5. Use of disposable cloths should be limited to two surfaces (i.e., use two treated cloths per ward, and two Administrative units can be cleaned with one cloth).

PROCEDURE

1. Assemble equipment. Take to assigned area.

2. Move furniture, if necessary.

3. Start dusting/sweeping at far end of room or area and work toward door.

4. Place floor tool on direct line with right toe. Hold handle loosely. Stand erect with feet about eight inches apart. Start dusting/sweeping floor-walking forward. Use a push stroke, lift tool at end of each stroke. Do not tap. Overlap each stroke.

5. Continue this procedure until area is completed. Clean under all stationary equipment and furniture.

6. Take up accumulated dirt. Use dustpan and counter brush. Place in plastic liner/trash bag on utility cart.

7. The dusting/sweeping procedure can be performed with the wet and dry vacuum cleaner. Dusting Isolation Units must be performed with vacuum.

8. Inspect work. Floor should not have any dust streaks. Replace furniture.

9. Clean equipment. Return to designated storage area. Discard disposable treated cloths. If broom bags are used, place in plastic liner/bag for laundering.

V. VACUUMING
(Wet and Dry)

PURPOSE: To remove dust and dirt and water, to control the spread of bacteria, to aid in reaching difficult-to-reach areas, and for appearance. This operation may be performed on floors, walls, ceiling, rugs, and carpets.

EQUIPMENT:
Upright or tank vacuum cleaner
Wet and dry vacuum cleaner
Attachments: Crevice tool, shelf brush, pipe brush, upholstery brush, walls and ceiling brush, dusting brush, and floor-dry and wet tools.

SAFETY PRECAUTIONS:

1. Empty vacuum when bag is half full.

2. If disposable bag is not in use, empty soil into plastic liner/bag.

3. Never position equipment so that it becomes a tripping hazard.

PROCEDURE

Dry

1. Assemble proper equipment and attachments for the area to be vacuumed:

   a. Upright vacuum for carpet

   b. Tank cleaner to use on floors, grooves, and high cleaning.

   c. Back-pack for stairs, hard to reach areas, walls and ceiling, and drapery.

2. Remove all furniture and other items interfering with the operation.

3. Start in farthest corner of room, area or top of item. Vacuum the surface in a back-and-forth motion.

4. Empty bag when half full. Continue this procedure until area or item is completed. Change attachments as required.

5. Replace furniture or items.

6. Take equipment to utility room. Empty and clean. Return to designated storage area.

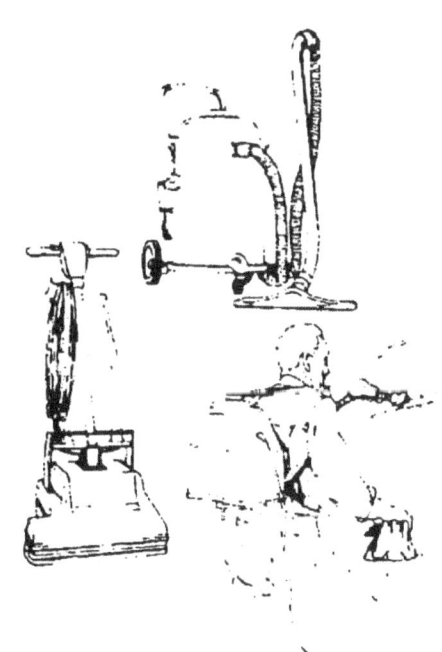

Wet

This procedure is used to remove water. It is considered very effective in the daily performance of different tasks in order to control the spread of infectious organisms. Wet vacuuming is often used in emergencies—flooding, pipe breaks, and overflows. See vacuum cleaning guide under Care of Equipment for operation of the wet vacuum.

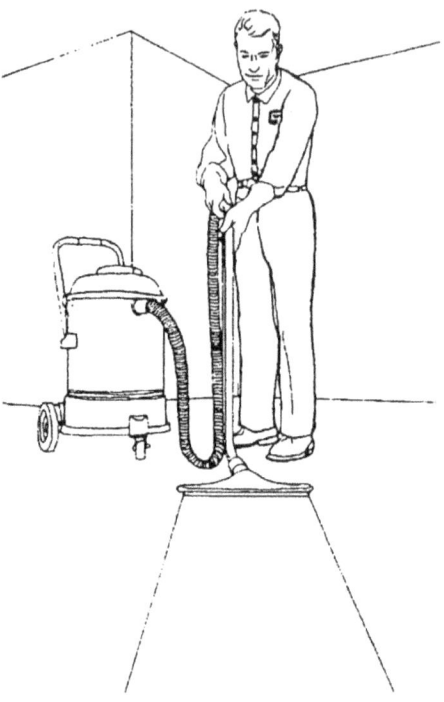

VI. MOPPING
(Wet, Damp, Spot)

PURPOSE: To insure maximum cleanliness, to improve the sanitation of the environment, to aid in control of bacteria, and for the appearance of the area.

EQUIPMENT:
    Utility cart
    Buckets (two)
    Dolly
    Wringers (two)
    Mopheads and handles (two)
    Nylon abrasive pad
    Caution signs
    Gloves
    Broom-Broom bags
    Sweeping tool-treated cloths
    Wet and dry vacuum cleaner
    Putty knife
    Dustpan
    Counter brush
    Germicidal detergent

SAFETY PRECAUTIONS:

1. Sweep or vacuum before mopping.

2. Post area with "Wet Floor" signs.

3. Mop one-half of corridor at a time.

4. Keep equipment close to walls and away from doors and corners.

5. Excessive water should not be allowed to remain on the floor for any length of time because it will cause damage to nearly all types of flooring material.

6. Begin the operation with clean equipment, mopheads, and clean solution.

7. Change cleaning solution and rinse water frequently (every three to four rooms, depending on size and soilage factors).

8. Solution containers should be conveniently positioned so as not to cause tripping or walking over cleaned areas.

PROCEDURE

Wet Mopping

1. Assemble equipment. Fill one container two-thirds full with water. Add recommended amount of germicidal detergent. Fill second container two-thirds full with clear water.

2. Proceed to designated work area. Post "Wet Floor" signs. Move furniture to simplify operation. Vacuum or dust area with covered broom or tool with treated cloth. Remove gum with putty knife. (Use dustpan and counter brush to remove debris and trash.)

3. Dip one mop into cleaning solution and press out excess water to prevent dripping.

4. First, apply solution on and along baseboard or coving. Use the heel of mophead to clean baseboard and corners. (The putty knife can be used to clean out heavily soiled corners or strands of the mophead wrapped around gloved fingertips is another tool for cleaning the corners. A baseboard scrubber or an improvised abrasive pad on a mop handle can be used to remove built-up soil on baseboards.)

5. Return mop to germicidal solution. Churn thoroughly, wring out and pick up solution off baseboards. Apply rinse water with second mop and dry.

6. Continue with the mopping operation. Take solution mop (with excess water pressed out) and make an eight-inch border around floor area approximately nine feet wide and twelve feet long.

7. Begin at top of area. Place mop flat on floor, feet well apart. Place right hand palm up, almost two inches from end of handle, and left hand palm down, about fourteen inches on handle. Begin swinging mop from left to right or right to left using a continuous open figure-eight motion. At the end of approximately six to nine strokes (width of strokes depend on height and weight of worker), turn mop over or renew direction by lapping mop (lift mophead and loop it over the strands). Continue this procedure until area is completed. (A nylon pad attached to one side of mophead can be used to remove black marks while performing the daily mopping procedure.)

8. Return mop to germicidal solution. Churn thoroughly. Wring out and pick up solution. Use same procedure as for applying solution.

9. Dip the second mop into the rinse water, press out excess water, and apply rinse water to area. Use same procedure for rinsing as for applying cleaning solution.

10. Dip the second mop again into rinse water, wring out thoroughly and dry floor using side-to-side stroke.

11. Continue the four steps of mopping, picking up, rinsing, and drying until the area has been covered. Change cleaning solution and rinse water frequently.

12. Inspect work; a properly mopped floor should have a clean surface. There should be no water spots. The corners should be clean and baseboards should not be splashed.

13. Wash and dry equipment and return to designated storage area.

14. Mophead are removed and placed in a plastic bag, and then placed in a regular laundry bag and stored in the designated area to be picked up and laundered.

Damp Mobbing

Damp mopping is a type of mopping used to remove surface dust. This procedure may be used in place of dry dust mopping. Each time mop is dipped into solution or rinse water, it is wrung out thoroughly. The same motions are carried out in this procedure as are for the wet mopping.

Spot Mopping

Spot mopping is a type of mopping used only when a small area is soiled by spillage (water, coke, coffee, urine, and other liquids). Spillage must be wiped up immediately in order to prevent slipping and falling hazards. First, absorb liquid with paper towels or blotters, then mop area.

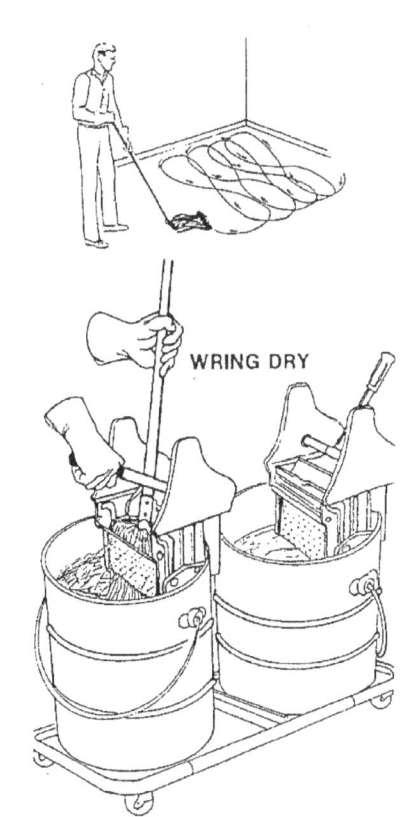

PHILOSOPHY, PRINCIPLES, PRACTICES, AND TECHNICS OF SUPERVISION, ADMINISTRATION, MANAGEMENT, AND ORGANIZATION

TABLE OF CONTENTS

	Page
MEANING OF SUPERVISION	1
THE OLD AND THE NEW SUPERVISION	1
THE EIGHT (8) BASIC PRINCIPLES OF THE NEW SUPERVISION	1
I. Principle of Responsibility	1
II. Principle of Authority	2
III. Principle of Self-Growth	2
IV. Principle of Individual Worth	2
V. Principle of Creative Leadership	2
VI. Principle of Success and Failure	2
VII. Principle of Science	3
VIII. Principle of Cooperation	3
WHAT IS ADMINISTRATION?	3
I. Practices Commonly Classed as "Supervisory"	3
II. Practices Commonly Classed as "Administrative"	3
III. Practices Commonly Classed as Both "Supervisory" and "Administrative"	4
RESPONSIBILITIES OF THE SUPERVISOR	4
COMPETENCIES OF THE SUPERVISOR	4
THE PROFESSIONAL SUPERVISOR-EMPLOYEE RELATIONSHIP	4
MINI-TEXT IN SUPERVISION, ADMINISTRATION, MANAGEMENT, AND ORGANIZATION	5
I. Brief Highlights	5
A. Levels of Management	6
B. What the Supervisor Must Learn	6
C. A Definition of Supervision	6
D. Elements of the Team Concept	6
E. Principles of Organization	6
F. The Four Important Parts of Every Job	7
G. Principles of Delegation	7
H. Principles of Effective Communications	7
I. Principles of Work Improvement	7
J. Areas of Job Improvement	7
K. Seven Key Points in Making Improvements	8

L.	Corrective Techniques for Job Improvement	8
M.	A Planning Checklist	8
N.	Five Characteristics of Good Directions	9
O.	Types of Directions	9
P.	Controls	9
Q.	Orienting the New Employee	9
R.	Checklist for Orienting New Employees	9
S.	Principles of Learning	10
T.	Causes of Poor Performance	10
U.	Four Major Steps in On-the-Job Instructions	10
V.	Employees Want Five Things	10
W.	Some Don'ts in Regard to Praise	11
X.	How to Gain Your Workers' Confidence	11
Y.	Sources of Employee Problems	11
Z.	The Supervisor's Key to Discipline	11
AA.	Five Important Processes of Management	12
BB.	When the Supervisor Fails to Plan	12
CC.	Fourteen General Principles of Management	12
DD.	Change	12

II. Brief Topical Summaries — 13
- A. Who/What is the Supervisor? — 13
- B. The Sociology of Work — 13
- C. Principles and Practices of Supervision — 14
- D. Dynamic Leadership — 14
- E. Processes for Solving Problems — 15
- F. Training for Results — 15
- G. Health, Safety, and Accident Prevention — 16
- H. Equal Employment Opportunity — 16
- I. Improving Communications — 16
- J. Self-Development — 17
- K. Teaching and Training — 17
    1. The Teaching Process — 17
        a. Preparation — 17
        b. Presentation — 18
        c. Summary — 18
        d. Application — 18
        e. Evaluation — 18
    2. Teaching Methods — 18
        a. Lecture — 18
        b. Discussion — 18
        c. Demonstration — 19
        d. Performance — 19
        e. Which Method to Use — 19

PHILOSOPHY, PRINCIPLES, PRACTICES, AND TECHNICS
OF
SUPERVISION, ADMINISTRATION, MANAGEMENT, AND ORGANIZATION

MEANING OF SUPERVISION

The extension of the democratic philosophy has been accompanied by an extension in the scope of supervision. Modern leaders and supervisors no longer think of supervision in the narrow sense of being confined chiefly to visiting employees, supplying materials, or rating the staff. They regard supervision as being intimately related to all the concerned agencies of society, they speak of the supervisor's function in terms of "growth," rather than the "improvement" of employees.

This modern concept of supervision may be defined as follows: Supervision is leadership and the development of leadership within groups which are cooperatively engaged in inspection, research, training, guidance, and evaluation.

THE OLD AND THE NEW SUPERVISION

TRADITIONAL
1. Inspection
2. Focused on the employee
3. Visitation
4. Random and haphazard
5. Imposed and authoritarian
6. One person usually

MODERN
1. Study and analysis
2. Focused on aims, materials, methods, supervisors, employees, environment
3. Demonstrations, intervisitation, workshops, directed reading, bulletins, etc.
4. Definitely organized and planned (scientific)
5. Cooperative and democratic
6. Many persons involved (creative)

THE EIGHT (8) BASIC PRINCIPLES OF THE NEW SUPERVISION

I. Principle of Responsibility
   Authority to act and responsibility for acting must be joined.
   A. If you give responsibility, give authority.
   B. Define employee duties clearly.
   C. Protect employees from criticism by others.
   D. Recognize the rights as well as obligations of employees.
   E. Achieve the aims of a democratic society insofar as it is possible within the area of your work.
   F. Establish a situation favorable to training and learning.
   G. Accept ultimate responsibility for everything done in your section, unit, office, division, department.
   H. Good administration and good supervision are inseparable.

II. Principle of Authority
The success of the supervisor is measured by the extent to which the power of authority is not used.
   A. Exercise simplicity and informality in supervision
   B. Use the simplest machinery of supervision
   C. If it is good for the organization as a whole, it is probably justified.
   D. Seldom be arbitrary or authoritative.
   E. Do not base your work on the power of position or of personality.
   F. Permit and encourage the free expression of opinions.

III. Principle of Self-Growth
The success of the supervisor is measured by the extent to which, and the speed with which, he is no longer needed.
   A. Base criticism on principles, not on specifics.
   B. Point out higher activities to employees.
   C. Train for self-thinking by employees to meet new situations.
   D. Stimulate initiative, self-reliance, and individual responsibility
   E. Concentrate on stimulating the growth of employees rather than on removing defects.

IV. Principle of Individual Worth
Respect for the individual is a paramount consideration in supervision.
   A. Be human and sympathetic in dealing with employees.
   B. Don't nag about things to be done.
   C. Recognize the individual differences among employees and seek opportunities to permit best expression of each personality.

V. Principle of Creative Leadership
The best supervision is that which is not apparent to the employee.
   A. Stimulate, don't drive employees to creative action.
   B. Emphasize doing good things.
   C. Encourage employees to do what they do best.
   D. Do not be too greatly concerned with details of subject or method.
   E. Do not be concerned exclusively with immediate problems and activities.
   F. Reveal higher activities and make them both desired and maximally possible.
   G. Determine procedures in the light of each situation but see that these are derived from a sound basic philosophy.
   H. Aid, inspire, and lead so as to liberate the creative spirit latent in all good employees.

VI. Principle of Success and Failure
There are no unsuccessful employees, only unsuccessful supervisors who have failed to give proper leadership.
   A. Adapt suggestions to the capacities, attitudes, and prejudices of employees.
   B. Be gradual, be progressive, be persistent.
   C. Help the employee find the general principle; have the employee apply his own problem to the general principle.
   D. Give adequate appreciation for good work and honest effort.
   E. Anticipate employee difficulties and help to prevent them.
   F. Encourage employees to do the desirable things they will do anyway.
   G. Judge your supervision by the results it secures.

VII. Principle of Science
Successful supervision is scientific, objective, and experimental. It is based on facts, not on prejudices.
- A. Be cumulative in results.
- B. Never divorce your suggestions from the goals of training.
- C. Don't be impatient of results.
- D. Keep all matters on a professional, not a personal, level.
- E. Do not be concerned exclusively with immediate problems and activities.
- F. Use objective means of determining achievement and rating where possible.

VIII. Principle of Cooperation
Supervision is a cooperative enterprise between supervisor and employee.
- A. Begin with conditions as they are.
- B. Ask opinions of all involved when formulating policies.
- C. Organization is as good as its weakest link.
- D. Let employees help to determine policies and department programs.
- E. Be approachable and accessible—physically and mentally.
- F. Develop pleasant social relationships.

WHAT IS ADMINISTRATION

Administration is concerned with providing the environment, the material facilities, and the operational procedures that will promote the maximum growth and development of supervisors and employees. (Organization is an aspect and a concomitant of administration.)

There is no sharp line of demarcation between supervision and administration; these functions are intimately interrelated and, often, overlapping. They are complementary activities.

I. Practices Commonly Classed as "Supervisory"
- A. Conducting employees' conferences
- B. Visiting sections, units, offices, divisions, departments
- C. Arranging for demonstrations
- D. Examining plans
- E. Suggesting professional reading
- F. Interpreting bulletins
- G. Recommending in-service training courses
- H. Encouraging experimentation
- I. Appraising employee morale
- J. Providing for intervisitation

II. Practices Commonly Classified as "Administrative"
- A. Management of the office
- B. Arrangement of schedules for extra duties
- C. Assignment of rooms or areas
- D. Distribution of supplies
- E. Keeping records and reports
- F. Care of audio-visual materials
- G. Keeping inventory records
- H. Checking record cards and books

I. Programming special activities
J. Checking on the attendance and punctuality of employees

III. Practices Commonly Classified as Both "Supervisory" and "Administrative"
   A. Program construction
   B. Testing or evaluating outcomes
   C. Personnel accounting
   D. Ordering instructional materials

RESPONSIBILITIES OF THE SUPERVISOR

A person employed in a supervisory capacity must constantly be able to improve his own efficiency and ability. He represent the employer to the employees and only continuous self-examination can make him a capable supervisor.

Leadership and training are the supervisor's responsibility. An efficient working unit is one in which the employees work with the supervisor. It is his job to bring out the best in his employees. He must always be relaxed, courteous, and calm in his association with his employees. Their feelings are important, and a harsh attitude does not develop the most efficient employees.

COMPETENCES OF THE SUPERVISOR

I. Complete knowledge of the duties and responsibilities of his position.
II. To be able to organize a job, plan ahead, and carry through.
III. To have self-confidence and initiative.
IV. To be able to handle the unexpected situation and make quick decisions.
V. To be able to properly train subordinates in the positions they are best suited for.
VI. To be able to keep good human relations among his subordinates.
VII. To be able to keep good human relations between his subordinates and himself and to earn their respect and trust.

THE PROFESSIONAL SUPERVISOR-EMPLOYEE RELATIONSHIP

There are two kinds of efficiency: one kind is only apparent and is produced in organizations through the exercise of mere discipline; this is but a simulation of the second, or true, efficiency which springs from spontaneous cooperation. If you are a manager, no matter how great or small your responsibility, it is your job, in the final analysis, to create and develop this involuntary cooperation among the people whom you supervise. For, no matter how powerful a combination of money, machines, and materials a company may have, this is a dead and sterile thing without a team of willing, thinking, and articulate people to guide it.

The following 21 points are presented as indicative of the exemplary basic relationship that should exist between supervisor and employee:

1. Each person wants to be liked and respected by his fellow employee and wants to be treated with consideration and respect by his superior.
2. The most competent employee will make an error. However, in a unit where good relations exist between the supervisor and his employees, tenseness and fear do not exist. Thus, errors are not hidden or covered up, and the efficiency of a unit is not impaired.

3. Subordinates resent rules, regulations, or orders that are unreasonable or unexplained.
4. Subordinates are quick to resent unfairness, harshness, injustices, and favoritism.
5. An employee will accept responsibility if he knows that he will be complimented for a job well done, and not too harshly chastised for failure; that his supervisor will check the cause of the failure, and, if it was the supervisor's fault, he will assume the blame therefore. If it was the employee's fault, his supervisor will explain the correct method or means of handling the responsibility.
6. An employee wants to receive credit for a suggestion he has made, that is used. If a suggestion cannot be used, the employee is entitled to an explanation. The supervisor should not say "no" and close the subject.
7. Fear and worry slow up a worker's ability. Poor working environment can impair his physical and mental health. A good supervisor avoids forceful methods, threats, and arguments to get a job done.
8. A forceful supervisor is able to train his employees individually and as a team, and is able to motivate them in the proper channels.
9. A mature supervisor is able to properly evaluate his subordinates and to keep them happy and satisfied.
10. A sensitive supervisor will never patronize his subordinates.
11. A worthy supervisor will respect his employees' confidences.
12. Definite and clear-cut responsibilities should be assigned to each executive.
13. Responsibility should always be coupled with corresponding authority.
14. No change should be made in the scope or responsibilities of a position without a definite understanding to that effect on the part of all persons concerned.
15. No executive or employee, occupying a single position in the organization, should be subject to definite orders from more than one source.
16. Orders should never be given to subordinates over the head of a responsible executive. Rather than do this, the officer in question should be supplanted.
17. Criticisms of subordinates should, whoever possible, be made privately, and in no case should a subordinate be criticized in the presence of executives or employees of equal or lower rank.
18. No dispute or difference between executives or employees as to authority or responsibilities should be considered too trivial for prompt and careful adjudication.
19. Promotions, wage changes, and disciplinary action should always be approved by the executive immediately superior to the one directly responsible.
20. No executive or employee should ever be required, or expected, to be at the same time an assistant to, and critic of, another.
21. Any executive whose work is subject to regular inspection should, wherever practicable, be given the assistance and facilities necessary to enable him to maintain an independent check of the quality of his work.

MINI-TEXT IN SUPERVISION, ADMINISTRATION, MANAGEMENT, AND ORGANIZATION

I. Brief Highlights

Listed concisely and sequentially are major headings and important data in the field for quick recall and review.

A. Levels of Management
Any organization of some size has several levels of management. In terms of a ladder, the levels are:

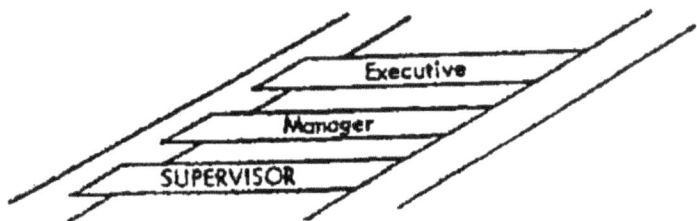

The first level is very important because it is the beginning point of management leadership.

B. What the Supervisor Must Learn
A supervisor must learn to:
1. Deal with people and their differences
2. Get the job done through people
3. Recognize the problems when they exist
4. Overcome obstacles to good performance
5. Evaluate the performance of people
6. Check his own performance in terms of accomplishment

C. A Definition of Supervisor
The term supervisor means any individual having authority, in the interests of the employer, to hire, transfer, suspend, lay-off, recall, promote, discharge, assign, reward, or discipline other employees or responsibility to direct them, or to adjust their grievances, or effectively to recommend such action, if, in connection with the foregoing, exercise of such authority is not of a merely routine or clerical nature but requires the use of independent judgment.

D. Elements of the Team Concept
What is involved in teamwork? The component parts are:
1. Members
2. A leader
3. Goals
4. Plans
5. Cooperation
6. Spirit

E. Principles of Organization
1. A team member must know what his job is.
2. Be sure that the nature and scope of a job are understood.
3. Authority and responsibility should be carefully spelled out.
4. A supervisor should be permitted to make the maximum number of decisions affecting his employees.
5. Employees should report to only one supervisor.
6. A supervisor should direct only as many employees as he can handle effectively.
7. An organization plan should be flexible.

8. Inspection and performance of work should be separate.
9. Organizational problems should receive immediate attention.
10. Assign work in line with ability and experience.

F. The Four Important Parts of Every Job
1. Inherent in every job is the *accountability* for results.
2. A second set of factors in every job is *responsibilities*.
3. Along with duties and responsibilities one must have the *authority* to act within certain limits without obtaining permission to proceed.
4. No job exists in a vacuum. The supervisor is surrounded by key *relationships*.

G. Principles of Delegation
Where work is delegated for the first time, the supervisor should think in terms of these questions:
1. Who is best qualified to do this?
2. Can an employee improve his abilities by doing this?
3. How long should an employee spend on this?
4. Are there any special problems for which he will need guidance?
5. How broad a delegation can I make?

H. Principles of Effective Communications
1. Determine the media.
2. To whom directed?
3. Identification and source authority.
4. Is communication understood?

I. Principles of Work Improvement
1. Most people usually do only the work which is assigned to them.
2. Workers are likely to fit assigned work into the time available to perform it.
3. A good workload usually stimulates output.
4. People usually do their best work when they know that results will be reviewed or inspected.
5. Employees usually feel that someone else is responsible for conditions of work, workplace layout, job methods, type of tools/equipment, and other such factors.
6. Employees are usually defensive about their job security.
7. Employees have natural resistance to change.
8. Employees can support or destroy a supervisor.
9. A supervisor usually earns the respect of his people through his personal example of diligence and efficiency.

J. Areas of Job Improvement
The areas of job improvement are quite numerous, but the most common ones which a supervisor can identify and utilize are:
1. Departmental layout
2. Flow of work
3. Workplace layout
4. Utilization of manpower
5. Work methods
6. Materials handling

7. Utilization
8. Motion economy

K. Seven Key Points in Making Improvements
1. Select the job to be improved
2. Study how it is being done now
3. Question the present method
4. Determine actions to be taken
5. Chart proposed method
6. Get approval and apply
7. Solicit worker participation

l. Corrective Techniques of Job Improvement
Specific Problems
1. Size of workload
2. Inability to meet schedules
3. Strain and fatigue
4. Improper use of men and skills
5. Waste, poor quality, unsafe conditions
6. Bottleneck conditions that hinder output
7. Poor utilization of equipment and machine
8. Efficiency and productivity of labor

General Improvement
1. Departmental layout
2. Flow of work
3. Work plan layout
4. Utilization of manpower
5. Work methods
6. Materials handling
7. Utilization of equipment
8. Motion economy

Corrective Techniques
1. Study with scale model
2. Flow chart study
3. Motion analysis
4. Comparison of units produced to standard allowance
5. Methods analysis
6. Flow chart and equipment study
7. Down time vs. running time
8. Motion analysis

M. A Planning Checklist
1. Objectives
2. Controls
3. Delegations
4. Communications
5. Resources
6. Manpower

7. Equipment
8. Supplies and materials
9. Utilization of time
10. Safety
11. Money
12. Work
13. Timing of improvements

N. Five Characteristics of Good Directions
In order to get results, directions must be:
1. Possible of accomplishment
2. Agreeable with worker interests
3. Related to mission
4. Planned and complete
5. Unmistakably clear

O. Types of Directions
1. Demands or direct orders
2. Requests
3. Suggestion or implication
4. volunteering

P. Controls
A typical listing of the overall areas in which the supervisor should establish controls might be:
1. Manpower
2. Materials
3. Quality of work
4. Quantity of work
5. Time
6. Space
7. Money
8. Methods

Q. Orienting the New Employee
1. Prepare for him
2. Welcome the new employee
3. Orientation for the job
4. Follow-up

R. Checklist for Orienting New Employees   Yes   No
1. Do you appreciate the feelings of new employees
   when they first report for work?   ___   ___
2. Are you aware of the fact that the new employee must
   make a big adjustment to his job?   ___   ___
3. Have you given him good reasons for liking the job and
   the organization?   ___   ___
4. Have you prepared for his first day on the job?   ___   ___
5. Did you welcome him cordially and make him feel needed?   ___   ___

	Yes	No

6. Did you establish rapport with him so that he feels free to talk and discuss matters with you? ___ ___
7. Did you explain his job to him and his relationship to you? ___ ___
8. Does he know that his work will be evaluated periodically on a basis that is fair and objective? ___ ___
9. Did you introduce him to his fellow workers in such a way that they are likely to accept him? ___ ___
10. Does he know what employee benefits he will receive? ___ ___
11. Does he understand the importance of being on the job and what to do if he must leave his duty station? ___ ___
12. Has he been impressed with the importance of accident prevention and safe practice? ___ ___
13. Does he generally know his way around the department? ___ ___
14. Is he under the guidance of a sponsor who will teach the right way of doing things? ___ ___
15. Do you plan to follow-up so that he will continue to adjust successfully to his job? ___ ___

S. Principles of Learning
 1. Motivation
 2. Demonstration or explanation
 3. Practice

T. Causes of Poor Performance
 1. Improper training for job
 2. Wrong tools
 3. Inadequate directions
 4. Lack of supervisory follow-up
 5. Poor communications
 6. Lack of standards of performance
 7. Wrong work habits
 8. Low morale
 9. Other

U. Four Major Steps in On-The-Job Instruction
 1. Prepare the worker
 2. Present the operation
 3. Tryout performance
 4. Follow-up

V. Employees Want Five Things
 1. Security
 2. Opportunity
 3. Recognition
 4. Inclusion
 5. Expression

W. Some Don'ts in Regard to Praise
1. Don't praise a person for something he hasn't done.
2. Don't praise a person unless you can be sincere.
3. Don't be sparing in praise just because your superior withholds it from you.
4. Don't let too much time elapse between good performance and recognition of it

X. How to Gain Your Workers' Confidence
Methods of developing confidence include such things as:
1. Knowing the interests, habits, hobbies of employees
2. Admitting your own inadequacies
3. Sharing and telling of confidence in others
4. Supporting people when they are in trouble
5. Delegating matters that can be well handled
6. Being frank and straightforward about problems and working conditions
7. Encouraging others to bring their problems to you
8. Taking action on problems which impede worker progress

Y. Sources of Employee Problems
On-the-job causes might be such things as:
1. A feeling that favoritism is exercised in assignments
2. Assignment of overtime
3. An undue amount of supervision
4. Changing methods or systems
5. Stealing of ideas or trade secrets
6. Lack of interest in job
7. Threat of reduction in force
8. Ignorance or lack of communications
9. Poor equipment
10. Lack of knowing how supervisor feels toward employee
11. Shift assignments

Off-the-job problems might have to do with:
1. Health
2. Finances
3. Housing
4. Family

Z. The Supervisor's Key to Discipline
There are several key points about discipline which the supervisor should keep in mind:
1. Job discipline is one of the disciplines of life and is directed by the supervisor.
2. It is more important to correct an employee fault than to fix blame for it.
3. Employee performance is affected by problems both on the job and off.
4. Sudden or abrupt changes in behavior can be indications of important employee problems.
5. Problems should be dealt with as soon as possible after they are identified.
6. The attitude of the supervisor may have more to do with solving problems than the techniques of problem solving.
7. Correction of employee behavior should be resorted to only after the supervisor is sure that training or counseling will not be helpful.

8. Be sure to document your disciplinary actions.
9. Make sure that you are disciplining on the basis of facts rather than personal feelings.
10. Take each disciplinary step in order, being careful not to make snap judgments, or decisions based on impatience.

AA. Five Important Processes of Management
1. Planning
2. Organizing
3. Scheduling
4. Controlling
5. Motivating

BB. When the Supervisor Fails to Plan
1. Supervisor creates impression of not knowing his job
2. May lead to excessive overtime
3. Job runs itself—supervisor lacks control
4. Deadlines and appointments missed
5. Parts of the work go undone
6. Work interrupted by emergencies
7. Sets a bad example
8. Uneven workload creates peaks and valleys
9. Too much time on minor details at expense of more important tasks

CC. Fourteen General Principles of Management
1. Division of work
2. Authority and responsibility
3. Discipline
4. Unity of command
5. Unity of direction
6. Subordination of individual interest to general interest
7. Remuneration of personnel
8. Centralization
9. Scalar chain
10. Order
11. Equity
12. Stability of tenure of personnel
13. Initiative
14. Esprit de corps

DD. Change

Bringing about change is perhaps attempted more often, and yet less well understood, than anything else the supervisor does. How do people generally react to change? (People tend to resist change that is imposed upon them by other individuals or circumstances.

Change is characteristic of every situation. It is a part of every real endeavor where the efforts of people are concerned.

1. Why do people resist change?
   People may resist change because of:
   a. Fear of the unknown
   b. Implied criticism
   c. Unpleasant experiences in the past
   d. Fear of loss of status
   e. Threat to the ego
   f. Fear of loss of economic stability

2. How can we best overcome the resistance to change?
   In initiating change, take these steps:
   a. Get ready to sell
   b. Identify sources of help
   c. Anticipate objections
   d. Sell benefits
   e. Listen in depth
   f. Follow up

II. Brief Topical Summaries

   A. Who/What is the Supervisor?
      1. The supervisor is often called the "highest level employee and the lowest level manager."
      2. A supervisor is a member of both management and the work group. He acts as a bridge between the two.
      3. Most problems in supervision are in the area of human relations, or people problems.
      4. Employees expect: Respect, opportunity to learn and to advance, and a sense of belonging, and so forth.
      5. Supervisors are responsible for directing people and organizing work. Planning is of paramount importance.
      6. A position description is a set of duties and responsibilities inherent to a given position.
      7. It is important to keep the position description up-to-date and to provide each employee with his own copy.

   B. The Sociology of Work
      1. People are alike in many ways; however, each individual is unique.
      2. The supervisor is challenged in getting to know employee differences. Acquiring skills in evaluating individuals is an asset.
      3. Maintaining meaningful working relationships in the organization is of great importance.
      4. The supervisor has an obligation to help individuals to develop to their fullest potential.
      5. Job rotation on a planned basis helps to build versatility and to maintain interest and enthusiasm in work groups.
      6. Cross training (job rotation) provides backup skills.

7. The supervisor can help reduce tension by maintaining a sense of humor, providing guidance to employees, and by making reasonable and timely decisions. Employees respond favorably to working under reasonably predictable circumstances.
8. Change is characteristic of all managerial behavior. The supervisor must adjust to changes in procedures, new methods, technological changes, and to a number of new and sometimes challenging situations.
9. To overcome the natural tendency for people to resist change, the supervisor should become more skillful in initiating change.

C. Principles and Practices of Supervision
1. Employees should be required to answer to only one superior.
2. A supervisor can effectively direct only a limited number of employees, depending upon the complexity, variety, and proximity of the jobs involved.
3. The organizational chart presents the organization in graphic form. It reflects lines of authority and responsibility as well as interrelationships of units within the organization.
4. Distribution of work can be improved through an analysis using the "Work Distribution Chart."
5. The "Work Distribution Chart" reflects the division of work within a unit in understandable form.
6. When related tasks are given to an employee, he has a better chance of increasing his skills through training.
7. The individual who is given the responsibility for tasks must also be given the appropriate authority to insure adequate results.
8. The supervisor should delegate repetitive, routine work. Preparation of recurring reports, maintaining leave and attendance records are some examples.
9. Good discipline is essential to good task performance. Discipline is reflected in the actions of employees on the job in the absence of supervision.
10. Disciplinary action may have to be taken when the positive aspects of discipline have failed. Reprimand, warning, and suspension are examples of disciplinary action.
11. If a situation calls for a reprimand, be sure it is deserved and remember it is to be done in private.

D. Dynamic Leadership
1. A style is a personal method or manner of exerting influence.
2. Authoritarian leaders often see themselves as the source of power and authority.
3. The democratic leader often perceives the group as the source of authority and power.
4. Supervisors tend to do better when using the pattern of leadership that is most natural for them.
5. Social scientists suggest that the effective supervisor use the leadership style that best fits the problem or circumstances involved.
6. All four styles—telling, selling, consulting, joining—have their place. Using one does not preclude using the other at another time.

7. The theory X point of view assumes that the average person dislikes work, will avoid it whenever possible, and must be coerced to achieve organizational objectives.
8. The theory Y point of view assumes that the average person considers work to be a natural as play, and, when the individual is committed, he requires little supervision or direction to accomplish desired objectives.
9. The leader's basic assumptions concerning human behavior and human nature affect his actions, decisions, and other managerial practices.
10. Dissatisfaction among employees is often present, but difficult to isolate. The supervisor should seek to weaken dissatisfaction by keeping promises, being sincere and considerate, keeping employees informed, and so forth.
11. Constructive suggestions should be encouraged during the natural progress of the work.

E. Processes for Solving Problems
1. People find their daily tasks more meaningful and satisfying when they can improve them.
2. The causes of problems, or the key factors, are often hidden in the background. Ability to solve problems often involves the ability to isolate them from their backgrounds. There is some substance to the cliché that some persons "can't see the forest for the trees."
3. New procedures are often developed from old ones. Problems should be broken down into manageable parts. New ideas can be adapted from old one.
4. People think differently in problem-solving situations. Using a logical, patterned approach is often useful. One approach found to be useful includes these steps:
   a. Define the problem
   b. Establish objectives
   c. Get the facts
   d. Weigh and decide
   e. Take action
   f. Evaluate action

F. Training for Results
1. Participants respond best when they feel training is important to them.
2. The supervisor has responsibility for the training and development of those who report to him.
3. When training is delegated to others, great care must be exercised to insure the trainer has knowledge, aptitude, and interest for his work as a trainer.
4. Training (learning) of some type goes on continually. The most successful supervisor makes certain the learning contributes in a productive manner to operational goals.
5. New employees are particularly susceptible to training. Older employees facing new job situations require specific training, as well as having need for development and growth opportunities.
6. Training needs require continuous monitoring.
7. The training officer of an agency is a professional with a responsibility to assist supervisors in solving training problems.

8. Many of the self-development steps important to the supervisor's own growth are equally important to the development of peers and subordinates. Knowledge of these is important when the supervisor consults with others on development and growth opportunities.

G. Health, Safety, and Accident Prevention
1. Management-minded supervisors take appropriate measures to assist employees in maintaining health and in assuring safe practices in the work environment.
2. Effective safety training and practices help to avoid injury and accidents.
3. Safety should be a management goal. All infractions of safety which are observed should be corrected without exception.
4. Employees' safety attitude, training and instruction, provision of safe tools and equipment, supervision, and leadership are considered highly important factors which contribute to safety and which can be influenced directly by supervisors.
5. When accidents do occur, they should be investigated promptly for very important reasons, including the fact that information which is gained can be used to prevent accidents in the future.

H. Equal Employment Opportunity
1. The supervisor should endeavor to treat all employees fairly, without regard to religion, race, sex, or national origin.
2. Groups tend to reflect the attitude of the leader. Prejudice can be detected even in very subtle form. Supervisors must strive to create a feeling of mutual respect and confidence in every employee.
3. Complete utilization of all human resources is a national goal. Equitable consideration should be accorded women in the work force, minority-group members, the physically and mentally handicapped, and the older employee. The important question is: "Who can do the job?"
4. Training opportunities, recognition for performance, overtime assignments, promotional opportunities, and all other personnel actions are to be handled on an equitable basis.

I. Improving Communications
1. Communications is achieving understanding between the sender and the receiver of a message. It also means sharing information—the creation of understanding.
2. Communication is basic to all human activity. Words are means of conveying meanings; however, real meanings are in people.
3. There are very practical differences in the effectiveness of one-way, impersonal, and two-way communications. Words spoken face-to-face are better understood. Telephone conversations are effective, but lack the rapport of person-to-person exchanges. The whole person communicates.
4. Cooperation and communication in an organization go hand in hand. When there is a mutual respect between people, spelling out rules and procedures for communicating is unnecessary.
5. There are several barriers to effective communications. These include failure to listen with respect and understanding, lack of skill in feedback, and misinterpreting the meanings of words used by the speaker. It is also common

practice to listen to what we want to hear, and tune out things we do not want to hear.
6. Communication is management's chief problem. The supervisor should accept the challenge to communicate more effectively and to improve interagency and intra-agency communications.
7. The supervisor may often plan for and conduct meetings. The planning phase is critical and may determine the success or the failure of a meeting.
8. Speaking before groups usually requires extra effort. Stage fright may never disappear completely, but it can be controlled.

J. Self-Development
1. Every employee is responsible for his own self-development.
2. Toastmaster and toastmistress clubs offer opportunities to improve skills in oral communications.
3. Planning for one's own self-development is of vital importance. Supervisors know their own strengths and limitations better than anyone else.
4. Many opportunities are open to aid the supervisor in his developmental efforts, including job assignments; training opportunities, both governmental and non-governmental—to include universities and professional conferences and seminars.
5. Programmed instruction offers a means of studying at one's own rate.
6. Where difficulties may arise from a supervisor's being away from his work for training, he may participate in televised home study or correspondence courses to meet his self-development needs.

K. Teaching and Training
1. The Teaching Process
Teaching is encouraging and guiding the learning activities of students toward established goals. In most cases this process consists of five steps: preparation, presentation, summarization, evaluation, and application.

   a. Preparation
   Preparation is two-fold in nature; that of the supervisor and the employee. Preparation by the supervisor is absolutely essential to success. He must know what, when, where, how, and whom he will teach. Some of the factors that should be considered are:
   1) The objectives
   2) The materials needed
   3) The methods to be used
   4) Employee participation
   5) Employee interest
   6) Training aids
   7) Evaluation
   8) Summarization

   Employee preparation consists in preparing the employee to receive the material. Probably the most important single factor in the preparation of the employee is arousing and maintaining his interest. He must know the objectives of the training, why he is there, how the material can be used, and its importance to him.

b. Presentation
   In presentation, have a carefully designed plan and follow it. The plan should be accurate and complete, yet flexible enough to meet situations as they arise. The method of presentation will be determined by the particular situation and objectives.

c. Summary
   A summary should be made at the end of every training unit and program. In addition, there may be internal summaries depending on the nature of the material being taught. The important thing is that the trainee must always be able to understand how each part of the new material relates to the whole.

d. Application
   The supervisor must arrange work so the employee will be given a chance to apply new knowledge or skills while the material is still clear in his mind and interest is high. The trainee does not really know whether he has learned the material until he has been given a chance to apply it. If the material is not applied, it loses most of its value.

e. Evaluation
   The purpose of all training is to promote learning. To determine whether the training has been a success or failure, the supervisor must evaluate this learning.
   In the broadest sense, evaluation includes all the devices, methods, skills, and techniques used by the supervisor to keep himself and the employees informed as to their progress toward the objectives they are pursuing. The extent to which the employee has mastered the knowledge, skills, and abilities, or changed his attitudes, as determined by the program objectives, is the extent to which instruction has succeeded or failed.
   Evaluation should not be confined to the end of the lesson, day, or program but should be used continuously. We shall note later the way this relates to the rest of the teaching process.

2. Teaching Methods
   A teaching method is a pattern of identifiable student and instructor activity used in presenting training material.
   All supervisors are faced with the problem of deciding which method should be used at a given time.

   a. Lecture
      The lecture is direct oral presentation of material by the supervisor. The present trend is to place less emphasis on the trainer's activity and more on that of the trainee.

   b. Discussion
      Teaching by discussion or conference involves using questions and other techniques to arouse interest and focus attention upon certain areas, and by doing so creating a learning situation. This can be one of the most

valuable methods because it gives the employees an opportunity to express their ideas and pool their knowledge.

    c. Demonstration
The demonstration is used to teach how something works or how to do something. It can be used to show a principle or what the results of a series of actions will be. A well-staged demonstration is particularly effective because it shows proper methods of performance in a realistic manner.

    d. Performance
Performance is one of the most fundamental of all learning techniques or teaching methods. The trainee may be able to tell how a specific operation should be performed but he cannot be sure he knows how to perform the operation until he has done so.
As with all methods, there are certain advantages and disadvantages to each method.

    e. Which Method to Use
Moreover, there are other methods and techniques of teaching. It is difficult to use any method without other methods entering into it. In any learning situation, a combination of methods is usually more effective than any one method alone.

Finally, evaluation must be integrated into the other aspects of the teaching-learning process.

It must be used in the motivation of the trainees; it must be used to assist in developing understanding during the training; and it must be related to employee application of the results of training.

This is distinctly the role of the supervisor.